Oliver Optic

All Adrift or the Goldwing Club

Oliver Optic

All Adrift or the Goldwing Club

ISBN/EAN: 9783743313415

Manufactured in Europe, USA, Canada, Australia, Japa

Cover: Foto ©ninafisch / pixelio.de

Manufactured and distributed by brebook publishing software (www.brebook.com)

Oliver Optic

All Adrift or the Goldwing Club

The Boat-Builder Series

ALL ADRIFT

OR

THE GOLDWING CLUB

BY

OLIVER OPTIC

AUTHOR OF "YOUNG AMERICA ABROAD" "THE GREAT WESTERN SERIES"
"THE ARMY AND NAVY SERIES" "THE WOODVILLE SERIES" "THE
STARRY-FLAG SERIES" "THE BOAT-CLUB STORIES" "THE
UPWARD AND ONWARD SERIES" "THE YACHT-CLUB
SERIES" "THE LAKE-SHORE SERIES" "THE
RIVERDALE STORIES" ETC. ETC.

WITH EIGHT ILLUSTRATIONS

BOSTON
LEE AND SHEPARD PUBLISHERS
NEW YORK
CHARLES T. DILLINGHAM
1883

COPYRIGHT, 1882,
BY WILLIAM T. ADAMS.

All rights reserved.

TO MY GRANDSON

ROBERT ELMER RUSSELL

This Book

IS AFFECTIONATELY DEDICATED.

PREFACE.

"ALL ADRIFT" is the first volume of a new set of books, to be known as "THE BOAT-BUILDER SERIES." The story contains the adventures of a boy who is trying to do something to help support the family, but who finds himself all adrift in the world. He has the reputation of being rather "wild," though he proves that he is honest, loves the truth, and is willing to work for a living. Having been born and brought up on the shore of Lake Champlain, he could not well avoid being a boatman, especially as his father was a pilot on a steamer. Nearly all the scenes of the story are on the water; and the boy shows not only that he can handle a boat, but that he has ingenuity, and fertility of resource.

The narrative of the hero's adventures contained in this volume is the introduction to the remaining volumes of the series, in which this boy and others are put in the way of obtaining a great deal of useful information, by which the readers of these books are expected to profit. Captain Royal Gildrock, a wealthy retired shipmaster, has some ideas of his own in regard to boys. He thinks that one great need of this country is educated mechanics, more skilled labor. He has the means to carry his ideas into practice, and actively engages in the work of instructing and building up the boys in a knowledge of the useful arts. He believes in religion, morality, and social and political virtue. He insists upon practice in addition to precept and theory, as well in the inculcation of the duties of social life as in mechanics and useful arts.

If the first volume is all story and adventure, those that follow it will not be wholly given up to the details of the mechanic arts. The captain has a steam-yacht; and the hero of the first story has a fine sailboat, to say nothing of a whole fleet of other craft belonging to the nabob. The boys are not of the tame sort: they are not of the humdrum kind, and they are inclined to make things lively. In fact, they are live boys, and the captain sometimes has his hands full in managing them.

With this explanation, the author sends out the first volume with the hope that this book and those which follow it will be as successful as their numerous predecessors in pleasing his young friends — and his old friends, he may add, as he treads the downhill of life.

DORCHESTER, MASS., Aug. 21, 1882.

CONTENTS.

CHAPTER I.
A Growling Passenger 13

CHAPTER II.
A Short and Decisive Conflict 24

CHAPTER III.
A Brilliant Scheme made Possible 34

CHAPTER IV.
In the Cabin of the Goldwing 45

CHAPTER V.
A Boat with a Bad Reputation 55

CHAPTER VI.
The Robbery at the Hotel 66

CHAPTER VII.
The Man that looked through the Keyhole . 76

CHAPTER VIII.
The Colchester Club changes its Name . . 87

CHAPTER IX.
A Weather Helm and a Lee Helm . . . 98

CONTENTS.

CHAPTER X.
The Missisquoi in Pursuit 109

CHAPTER XI.
The Beginning of the Chase 119

CHAPTER XII.
A Rough Time of it 129

CHAPTER XIII.
Safe under a Lee 140

CHAPTER XIV.
Early in the Morning 150

CHAPTER XV.
The Strategy of the Chase 161

CHAPTER XVI.
A Grave Charge against the Skipper . . . 172

CHAPTER XVII.
Dory Dornwood decides to "face the Music" . 183

CHAPTER XVIII.
Dory locks his Passengers into the Cabin . . 194

CHAPTER XIX.
Pearl Hawlinshed resorts to Violence . . 205

CHAPTER XX.
Mr. Peppers finds the Tables turned . . . 215

CHAPTER XXI.
Another Element in the Contest 226

CONTENTS. xi

CHAPTER XXII.
PAGE
THE GAME AMONG THE SHALLOWS 237

CHAPTER XXIII.
HEADED OFF ON BOTH SIDES 247

CHAPTER XXIV.
THROUGH VARIED STRIFE AND STRUGGLES . . . 257

CHAPTER XXV.
WIND SOUTH-SOUTH-WEST BLOWING FRESH . . 268

CHAPTER XXVI.
DORY DORNWOOD MANŒUVRES TO ESCAPE . . . 278

CHAPTER XXVII.
DORY MAKES A HARBOR FOR THE NIGHT . . . 289

CHAPTER XXVIII.
TERRIBLE INTELLIGENCE FROM HOME 300

CHAPTER XXIX.
CAPTAIN GILDROCK HAS DECIDED OBJECTIONS . . 310

CHAPTER XXX.
CAPTAIN GILDROCK DILATES UPON HIS NOTABLE
SCHEME 321

ALL ADRIFT;

OR,

THE GOLDWING CLUB.

CHAPTER I.

A GROWLING PASSENGER.

"BOY, I told you to bring me some pickles," said Major Billcord, a passenger on a Lake Champlain steamer, to a boy in a white jacket, who was doing duty as a waiter at dinner in the cabin.

"Yes, sir; and I brought them," replied Dory Dornwood, as he took the dish of pickles almost from under the passenger's nose, and placed it quite under his nose.

"No impudence to me, boy!" exclaimed Major Billcord, as he bestowed a savage glance at the young waiter.

"I beg your pardon, sir: I did not mean to be impudent," replied Dory meekly.

"Waiter, bring me a piece of roast beef rare. Now, mind, I want it rare," said the passenger sitting next to the major.

"Yes, sir; in a moment, sir," added Dory, to indicate that he heard the order.

"When I send you for any thing, you should put it where I can see it," added Major Billcord sternly.

"I thought I put the pickles where you could see them," answered Dory, as he started for the pantry to obtain the roast beef rare.

"Here, boy, stop!" called the major. "Where are you going now? Bring me the boiled onions, and I want them well done."

"Yes, sir," replied the waiter, as he darted after the onions, and returned with them in an instant; for he found the dish in another part of the table. "The boiled onions," he added, as he placed them beside the snappy passenger's plate, so that he should be sure to see them.

"Isn't it about time for my roast beef, waiter?" asked the next gentleman.

"In a moment, sir."

"These onions are not half done, boy!" exclaimed the major. "I told you to bring me onions well done, and not raw onions."

"I don't cook them, sir; and I brought such as I find on the table," pleaded Dory, as he started to fill the order of the next passenger.

"Here! come back, boy! I want boiled onions well done, and I don't want any impudence," snarled the major.

Dory brought another dish of onions, and placed them by the side of the gentleman's plate. He repeated the order of the next passenger to assure him that he had not forgotten it, and was in the act of rushing for it, when Major Billcord broke out again.

"These onions are no better than the others: they are not half cooked. Now go to the steward, and tell him I want boiled onions well done."

"Get my roast beef first," added the next passenger.

"Here, waiter! bring me a sidebone of chicken, some green pease, string-beans, pickled beets, boiled cabbage, a plate of macaroni, and any other vegetables you may happen to have; and don't be all day about it," said the passenger on the other side of Major Billcord.

"In a minute, sir," replied Dory.

"Go to the steward at once, and tell him what I want," stormed the major.

"Waiter, bring me a plate of roast stuffed veal, with a specimen of all the vegetables on the bill of fare. Don't leave out any. If you leave out any of them, I will travel by railroad the next time I go north," shouted another passenger.

Dory did not wait to hear any more. He was not a waiter of great experience, and he found that the confusion of orders was rather trying to him. He went to the carving-table, delivered the message of Major Billcord to the steward, and called for the orders he had received. Before he had his tray ready, the steward brought him the onions; and he carried them with the other articles to the table.

"Your onions, sir," said he, as he placed the little dish where the irate gentleman could not help seeing them.

While Dory was serving the other passengers, whose orders he had taken, and while half a dozen others were clamorous for every item on the bill of fare, Major Billcord thrust his fork into one of the odoriferous vegetables brought to him.

"These are not a whit better done than the others were!" exclaimed Major Billcord, dropping his knife and fork in disgust. "What do you mean, boy, by bringing me such onions as these?"

"The steward gave me those onions for you, sir," pleaded Dory, who was certainly doing his best to please all the passengers at the dinner-table; and the young waiter had already learned that this was not one of the easiest tasks in the world.

"Don't tell me that, you young rascal! You haven't delivered my message to the steward," growled the irate passenger.

"Yes, sir: I told him just what you wanted, and he sent the dish of onions to you, sir," Dory explained.

"The steward would never have sent me such onions as these. You haven't been to him as I told you. You are an impudent young cub, and you are no more fit for a waiter than you are for a steamboat captain."

"I brought the onions the steward sent; and it

isn't my fault that they are not right," said Dory gently, though he did not always speak and act in just that way.

"Is my dinner to be spoiled by the stupidity and carelessness of a boy?" demanded Major Billcord. "If I have any influence on board of this boat, such blockheads shall not be employed as waiters."

"I will get any thing you wish, sir," added Dory, appalled at the remark of the important passenger.

"Don't come near me again! Go, and tell the steward to send another waiter to me," was all the reply the major would give him.

Dory Dornwood intended to deliver even this message to the steward; but he was kept very busy by the wants of the other passengers, so that he could not go at just that minute. He had been instructed to serve all persons at the tables alike; and he was not quite old enough and experienced enough to comprehend that his instructions were to be obeyed in a Pickwickian sense on certain occasions.

Major Billcord sat back in his chair, and watched the movements of the boy-waiter for the full space of fifteen seconds, which he doubtless interpreted as fifteen minutes. It was not to be expected that he could finish, or even go on with, his dinner without the boiled onions well done. Possibly he did not care so much for the aromatic vegetable as he did for his own sweet will. At any rate, he would not touch another morsel of food; and, when the fifteen seconds had fully expired, he was ready to make another demonstration.

"Boy, didn't I tell you to go and call the steward, and tell him to send me another waiter?" demanded Major Billcord, as savagely as though Dory had struck him in the face.

"Yes, sir, you did, and I am going; but we are all very busy, and the passengers want a great many things. I am going now, sir," replied Dory, who thought it might be safer to let the rest of the passengers wait than to anger so great a magnate as the major.

Dory delivered his message, and the steward uttered an exclamation which would have cost him his situation if Major Billcord had heard it. The head of the culinary department went to the place occupied by the important personage.

"If you don't discharge that boy before supper-time, there will be trouble," said the major when the steward presented himself. "He is stupid, careless, and impertinent. He had the presumption to tell me that he did not cook the onions, and it was not his fault that they were not properly done."

Possibly the steward might have voted on the same side of the question, if he had considered it prudent to express an opinion; but he apologized for the cook, and said nothing about the waiter. He explained that he had been to the kitchen for the onions, and had sent the best on the boat to the distinguished passenger.

"Then the young rascal gave them to some other person!" exclaimed Major Billcord. "The boy is not fit for a waiter."

"He is only serving for a week or two, while one of our regular waiters is away. He is the son of one of the second pilots."

"Which one?" demanded the angry passenger.

"Dornwood. He says the boy is a little wild, and he wants to get something for him to do," added the steward. "The boy is rather more than his mother can manage when his father is away, as he is all the season."

"This is not a reform-school, and we don't want any such scallawags on the boat. But you needn't tell Dornwood that I said any thing about his boy," added the major in a low tone.

Of course the steward would not say any thing on such a delicate subject. After dinner Dory Dornwood was called up and discharged. He tried to explain that he had done his best, and had not spoken an impudent word. The steward had been satisfied with him, but it was impossible to resist the influence of such a man as Major Billcord.

Perry Dornwood was the second pilot of one of the night boats for this week; and Dory could not run to his father with his grievance, for he felt that he had a grievance. Possibly it would have done no good if he had. His father had had some trouble with him, and he was more inclined to believe the worst that could be said of his son than the best.

Perry Dornwood the pilot had rather forced himself into the position he occupied. He was a good enough pilot; but he drank too much whiskey to be fully reliable. He was never drunk, at least not when on duty; but he was generally pretty well soaked in liquor. The captain of his steamer did not believe in him, and Perry's position had been nearly lost several times; but some kind of an influence still kept him in his place.

The pilot lived in Burlington. He had a wife and two children, a son and a daughter. Mrs. Dornwood was a most excellent woman, but she was almost discouraged under the trials and difficulties which beset her path in life. Her husband did not half provide for his little family; and it was all the poor mother could do to scrub along, feeding and clothing the boy and girl.

The pilot had work only a portion of the year on the lake, and he was not disposed to find other employment when not so engaged. Even the money he did earn did not all find its way into the expenditures for taking care of the family. It was feared by the good woman that her husband gambled.

Dory—his name was Theodore—was now fourteen years old. His mother had explained to him the condition of the family finances. They had nothing, and Perry Dornwood owed many debts.

The boy had been wild, but those who knew him best said there was nothing bad about him. He had looked for work, and his father had found it for him. Now he had lost his place; and his discharge was a very heavy blow to him, though he was wild.

CHAPTER II.

A SHORT AND DECISIVE CONFLICT.

DORY DORNWOOD appeared to be in no hurry to get home after his discharge. The steamer stopped at Burlington after his fate had been decided, and the steward expected him to take his things on shore. The ex-waiter evidently had other views, for he kept out of sight until after the boat had left the wharf.

When the steamer reached Plattsburg, Dory Dornwood went on shore. He visited all the hotels in the place, and endeavored to obtain a situation as a waiter, or as any thing else — he did not care what — by which he could earn some money to help support the family. He could obtain no situation, though he heard of a place a few miles out in the country where a boy was wanted. Dory had no money, — not a penny; for his father collected his wages. He decided to visit the place at once, so as to be the first to apply for the position.

After he had walked a couple of miles, and had one more to go, he came to a piece of woods through which the road extended. He began to feel very tired, for he had done a day's work before he landed from the steamer. It was now nearly eight o'clock in the evening. He had eaten no supper, and not much dinner; for the events in the cabin had taken off his appetite. With no money and no friends, he was not very clear as to where his supper was to come from. The question of a lodging was involved in quite as much doubt.

The weather was warm; and, if he was compelled to lodge in the woods, it would not be the first time he had slept in the open air. Though he had rather more than his fair share of pride, any farmer would give him a meal of victuals for the asking. But just now he was tired, and he wanted rest. He walked a short distance from the road, and seated himself on a rock. It was not comfortable; and he stretched his body upon the ground, which was covered with a clean carpet of fine needles.

Of course he could not help thinking of the great event of the day; and, while he was considering it, he fell asleep. Possibly his slumber continued an hour; and it might have continued another hour, or even all night, if he had not been disturbed by footsteps near him. The nails in the heel of a heavy boot grated upon a flat rock, and this was the noise that awakened the tired sleeper.

Dory half rose from his reclining posture, and discovered a man moving stealthily towards the road. He was creeping with the utmost care: and probably the scraping of his boot against the rock had admonished him to be more careful; at any rate he acted as though such were the case.

The seeker for a situation was wide awake as soon as he was awake at all. He sat on the ground watching the stranger as he crawled towards the road. It was quite dark, but the opening made by the highway admitted some light from the stars. Dory thought the stranger had something in his hand. If the man had walked right along, the boy would have thought nothing of the fact that he was in the woods after dark; but he was creeping like a cat, and Dory's curiosity was aroused.

He got upon his feet, and walked after the

mysterious stranger. He did not care to show himself, and he kept one of the big trees between himself and the man all the time. Near the road a fringe of bushes had sprung up, and in their foliage the man concealed himself. Dory had obtained a better view of what the stranger had in his hand; and, though he was not sure of it, he thought it was a gun. Was the man out hunting in the dark? There were no deer so near the town, and it was hardly likely that the person was gunning in the darkness.

Dory continued to creep from tree to tree until he could not have been more than a couple of rods from the concealed night wanderer. If he had not believed the man had a gun in his hand, he would have left his concealment and gone about his business; for he had come to the conclusion that the affair, whatever it was, did not concern him. But he felt a little bashful about leaving, lest the gun might go off, and the shot accidentally strike him.

The next minute he was confident that he heard footsteps in the road. Before he had time to satisfy himself fully on this point, the gun in the hand of the stranger went off; and its going-off proved to Dory that it was a gun, as he had supposed, and even believed.

"Help! help!" shouted some one in the road; and the voice proved that there was some one there.

Scarcely had the word been uttered before the man in the bushes broke from his place of concealment, and rushed towards the road. Dory was too much interested in the affair to remain at a distance any longer. It was none of his business; but it was plain enough that the mysterious stranger had fired his gun at the person who shouted for assistance from the road. Dory reasoned, that, as he had fired the gun once, he could not fire it again without reloading it; and he had not had time to do this.

But there was some sort of wickedness in progress, and Dory ran with all his might to the road; and, even if he had not run with all his might, it would not have taken him a great while to accomplish two rods. When he came to the opening, he saw one man spring upon another. The former dropped the gun he carried in his hand, and it was plain that he had fired the shot.

The two men clutched each other, though one

of them tried to say something to the other. Dory had lots of blood in his veins, and it began to boil as though it was over a hot fire. All his sympathies were with the man who had been attacked. The other had crept upon him like a thief in the night, had fired at him, and then had followed up the attack with a hand-to-hand onslaught.

"Don't, Pearl!" pleaded the man who had been attacked. "Consider what you are doing! You will ruin yourself! You are sure to be discovered, even if you kill me!"

Dory did not wait to hear any more. He had a strong impulse to take a hand in the affair, though it was none of his business. The stranger who had wakened him from his slumbers was back to him, and the boy thought his opportunity at the present instant was too good to be lost.

The supperless wanderer flung himself upon the shoulders of the assailant, and grappled him around the throat with all his strength. He was well aware, that, if he failed at the first dash, his chance would not only be gone, but he would be in danger of being entirely wiped out by his intended victim.

Dory was not a very heavy boy, but he was remarkably active. He dug his knees into the back of the man, and in a moment he brought him to the ground. The stranger then turned his attention to his assailant, and he made short work of him. He seemed only to shake himself, and Dory went half way across the road.

The ex-waiter was on his feet again in an instant. He looked at the assailant, and saw that he had a sort of cloth mask on his face. As the boy sprang to his feet, the stranger was in the act of picking up his gun. He snatched it from the ground, and then fled into the woods. The conflict appeared to be ended.

Dory puffed like a fish out of water. He had been laboring under tremendous excitement, which is not at all strange; for it would have stirred the blood of any one to see another attacked with a deadly weapon.

Dory watched the woods, and rather expected that a bullet would soon be travelling from that direction towards him and the person who had been attacked. But his companion in the road did not seem to be at all alarmed: at least he did not make any haste to seek a safer position.

"It is dangerous being safe just here," said Dory, when he had collected his scattered thoughts, and realized that it was time something was done. "I think we had better move on, or that gun will go off again."

"I don't think it will go off again," replied the man in the road, in a very sad, rather than an alarmed or indignant tone.

"Didn't that man fire at you? Won't he do it again?" demanded Dory.

"I don't think he intended to hit me; though he fired at me, or he fired his gun. I don't believe he fired it at me," answered the stranger in a confused manner.

"If he fired at you, of course he meant to hit you. What in the world should he fire at you for if he didn't mean to hit you?" asked Dory, wondering at the reasoning of his companion in the road.

"I am confident I am right; but we won't say any thing more about it just now," added the stranger, who seemed to be struggling with other emotions than those of fear or indignation.

"That's very queer," said Dory, puzzled at the strange conduct of the man who had been fired at. "I think you will get a bullet through your head if you stay here much longer."

"I am not afraid of a bullet; but I don't think I had better stay here any longer," replied the stranger. "Which way are you going, young man?"

"I was going over to a place they call Belzer's."

"That is a mile from here. Were you going there when that gun was fired?" asked the man eagerly.

"Well, not just at that minute. I was tired out, and I lay down in the woods to rest me. I was going over to Belzer's to see if I could get a place to work. I"—

"You are too late: they hired a boy at Belzer's this afternoon," added the man.

"That's just my luck," added Dory, discouraged at this intelligence.

"The luck shall not go against you this time. You have no errand at Belzer's now; and, if you will walk to Plattsburgh with me, I will make it all right with you; and you shall not be sorry that you did not find a place at Belzer's, which is not a proper place for a boy like you."

"If there is no place there for me, and it is not the place for me, I shall return to Plattsburgh," answered Dory, as he started with the stranger in the direction from which he had come when he took to the woods.

In a short time they came out into the open country; and there was no longer any danger that the attack from the mysterious assailant would be renewed.

"Young man, you have done me a great service; and you have done a greater one to another person," said the stranger.

"Who's that?" asked Dory, puzzled by the strange speech of his companion.

"I mean the one who fired the gun at me," answered his fellow-traveller.

"That's funny!" exclaimed Dory. "You and he seem to be fooling with each other. He shot at you, and didn't mean to hit you; and now I have done him a great service. I suppose you don't mean to pay me for the service I did him," laughed Dory.

"I should be willing to pay you more for what you did for him than for what you did for me."

Dory was bewildered.

CHAPTER III.

A BRILLIANT SCHEME MADE POSSIBLE.

DORY began to think his companion was a lunatic. Certainly he was a Christian man, for he seemed to have nothing but kindness in his heart towards his late assailant.

"I don't want any pay for what I did for either," said Dory Dornwood, as he saw his companion thrust his hand into his pocket, and he feared that his joke had been taken in earnest.

"We will talk about that when we get to Plattsburgh. Will you tell me your name, young man?"

"My name is Theodore Dornwood, though almost everybody calls me Dory. But I don't care what they call me, if they don't call me too late to supper, or don't call me at all, as nobody did to-night," replied Dory. And an emphatic wrenching at his stomach, just at the moment he spoke, compelled him to repeat that ancient witticism.

"You have had no supper, Dory?" demanded his new friend, with much sympathy in his tones.

"Not a bit, and not much dinner," added Dory. "Major Billcord spoiled my dinner. And I dare say he charges me with spoiling his dinner: but I didn't; it was the cook."

The curiosity of his companion was excited, and Dory told the whole story of his experience as a waiter at dinner that day. In answering the questions of the stranger, he told the history of himself and his family. He enlarged upon his efforts to obtain a situation, and declared that he wanted to do something to help his mother, and make things easier for her.

Just as he was finishing his narrative, they reached the front of a farmhouse. The stranger led the way to the door, and knocked. Presently the door was opened by a man with a lamp in his hand. Dory wondered what his companion wanted there; for he had not spoken of making a call on the way to the town.

"Ah! is that you, Basil Hawlinshed?" said the occupant of the house, as the light from his lamp fell upon the face of the stranger, — a stranger to Dory, though he did not appear to be such to the man of the house. "I am glad to see you. Come in!"

"Thank you, Neighbor Brookbine. I am sorry to trouble you: but this young man with me has not been to supper yet; and it makes my stomach turn somersets to travel with any one who has not been to supper when it is after nine o'clock in the evening."

"Come in! come in, Neighbor Hawlinshed! though I suppose you are to be no longer my neighbor. The boy shall have the best supper we can get up for him at this time of night."

Mr. Hawlinshed — for this appeared to be the name to which he answered — and Dory followed him into the house. When he had gone to make preparations for the supper, Dory's companion led him to one side of the room.

"Will you do me a favor, Dory?" said Mr. Hawlinshed.

"I will try with all my might to do it," replied Dory.

"Don't say one word about what happened in the woods while you are in this house," said Mr. Hawlinshed earnestly, and with much emotion.

"Oh, that's an easy one!" replied Dory gayly. "I could do that, and only half try."

"Be very sure you don't speak a word about the matter, or even hint at it in the most distant manner," continued Mr. Hawlinshed with painful emphasis.

"Not a word or a hint, sir. No one shall squeeze it out of me with a cider-press," protested Dory.

Mr. Brookbine came into the room, and Mr. Hawlinshed tried to compose himself. The talk of the two men was upon subjects in which the boy felt no interest. He was more concerned about his supper than about the affairs of the two speakers. But he learned that Mr. Hawlinshed had been a farmer, and had just sold his farm for forty-five hundred dollars in cash. He was going to another part of the State to engage in the lumber business.

Nothing was said which afforded Dory a clew to the strange event in the woods. He fancied it had some connection with the money the farmer had received for his farm. The hungry boy was called into another room by Mrs. Brookbine to eat his supper. He found a plentiful meal on the table, and he did ample justice to it. While he was eating, the farmer's wife, who was a motherly sort of woman, plied him with questions; and he answered all those that related to himself, but he was extremely careful not to betray the confidence of his new friend.

Dory felt like a new creature when he had finished his supper, which he thought was quite good enough to have suited Major Billcord; though he was sure that it would not have suited him, for the simple reason that he was never suited with any thing. Mr. Hawlinshed offered to pay for the meal, and Farmer Brookbine felt insulted by the proposition. The visitor explained that he should not have offered to pay for his own supper, but he had brought an entire stranger into the house. Mr. Brookbine declared that he always gave a meal of victuals to any one who needed it. With many thanks the visitors took their leave, and resumed their walk to town. In less than half an hour they were at a hotel in Plattsburgh.

"I can't stay here, Mr. Hawlinshed," said Dory, as they entered the house. "I have no money to pay my bill."

"Do you think I am a heathen, that I won't pay

your bill after the service you have done me?" asked Mr. Hawlinshed with a smile.

"I don't want anybody to pay for me," protested Dory.

"Don't talk so, my boy," added his new friend. "Come to my room, for I want to talk with you."

Dory assented, though he had set his teeth against taking any thing that looked like charity. He followed Mr. Hawlinshed up-stairs, where it appeared that he had a room. It contained a trunk, a valise, and other baggage.

"Dory, you have rendered me a service that you cannot understand; and I am glad you cannot. I should feel mean to the end of my life if I did not attempt to make some slight return for it," said Mr. Hawlinshed, as he seated himself at a table. "I don't think you saved my life, for I don't believe my life was in danger for a moment."

"I don't think I saved your life, but I think your life has been in danger. Why, the fellow might have hit you by accident, even if he didn't mean to," replied Dory. "But the villain went at you as though he meant to tear you in pieces after he had fired the gun."

"It is hardly worth while to argue the question. I am very confident of what I say. My life has not been in danger, but my money was in great peril. I had forty-seven hundred and fifty dollars in my pocket when that person attacked me," continued Mr. Hawlinshed.

"Jerusalem!" exclaimed Dory, who did not remember that he had ever before been near so much money in all his life.

"I should have lost that money if you had not saved it, Dory. This was the point I was coming to. Don't ask me any questions, for I don't want to answer them."

"I won't ask any, if you don't want me to," added Dory, who was very much mystified by the occurrences of the evening.

"So far as I know and believe, you are the only person who saw the affair in the woods. The three who took part in the affray are the only persons on earth who know any thing about it," added Mr. Hawlinshed.

"I did not see or hear anybody around while I was in the woods," replied Dory. "I don't believe anybody else knows about it."

"That is very lucky, and I am only sorry that

you happened to witness the sad affair. Now, Dory, I don't want any other person to know any thing about it."

"Nobody shall find out any thing about it from me," protested the boy. "You used me very handsomely, and got a good supper for me when I should have had to feed on wind if I hadn't come across you."

Mr. Hawlinshed looked the boy in the face; for he suspected that Dory was making game of him when he weighed so insignificant a thing as a supper against the help he had given him in the woods. He took out a large pocket-book, which appeared to be filled with bank-bills. From them he selected several bills, and tendered them to Dory.

"What's that?" asked the boy, as he looked suspiciously at the bills. "I don't want any money for any thing I have done."

"Here is one hundred and five dollars," continued Mr. Hawlinshed. "The five dollars is to pay any expenses you may incur in getting home, so that you may have the hundred when you get there."

Dory looked at the money, and the temptation

to take it was very great. He could not bring himself to accept money for doing a kind act to a person who needed his assistance. On this ground he stoutly refused to touch the bills.

"Not for saving my life or preventing me from being hurt, Dory, but for saving my money. I shall be very unhappy, and feel mean, if you don't take the money. If I were rich, I should insist upon your taking thousands. This is a very small sum for the service you have rendered, for saving me from a loss which would have defeated the business enterprise I have in view. Take it, Dory, for my sake, if not for your own. It will be a great help to your mother," persisted Mr. Hawlinshed.

It looked easier to Dory than at first. He had saved his companion's money, and prevented him from losing forty-seven hundred and fifty dollars. But it took another half an hour of argument to satisfy Dory that he was not doing a mean thing in taking the bills. He took them at last, and his companion seemed to be happy in the fact that he had done so.

Dory felt rich enough to buy out the New York Central Railroad, or to become the proprietor of half the land that bordered on Lake Champlain. He had an idea of buying out the steamer on which Major Billcord had caused his discharge. At any rate, he must buy out something that would float on the lake, for he was about half boy and half boat.

He put the money into the old wallet he carried; and he doubted if all the money it had ever contained, even before it came into his possession, would equal the amount he had just deposited in one of its compartments. He had scarcely returned the treasure to his pocket, before he thought of the use to which he would apply the whole or a part of the money. It was a brilliant scheme. He had nursed it in his imagination as an unattainable enterprise, but now the money in his pocket rendered it possible.

"I feel better now, Dory," said Mr. Hawlinshed. "I have given you a feather's weight where I owe you a ton, but I hope the time will come when I can do better. I am going to write a letter now, and I want you to deliver it for me to-morrow. Will you do so?"

"To be sure I will," replied Dory warmly.

"I shall leave by the boat going south in the

morning; and I want this letter delivered after I am gone," added Mr. Hawlinshed, as he began to write on a sheet of paper on the table.

Dory considered his brilliant scheme.

CHAPTER IV.

IN THE CABIN OF THE GOLDWING.

"HERE is the letter, Dory," said Mr. Hawlinshed when he had sealed and directed the envelope. "You will have to go about a mile beyond the place where we met last night. Mr. Pearl Hawlinshed," he added, reading the address upon the letter.

"Pearl!" repeated Dory, as he took the letter and read the name for himself.

"That is the name; and the person to whom it is addressed is my son," replied the writer of the missive.

"Your son!" exclaimed Dory, looking intently into the face of his new friend.

"Yes: is there any thing very strange about that? He is my only son, my only child; and his mother has been dead many years."

"Your son!" repeated Dory, as though he was unable to comprehend the relation.

"Pearl Hawlinshed; and he is my son. Is there any thing very strange about it?" asked the father, looking anxiously at Dory.

"But he is the man who fired the gun at you, and then pitched into you," added Dory.

Mr. Hawlinshed manifested a great deal of emotion. He dropped into his chair, from which he had risen when he finished his letter. He appeared to be greatly astonished that his companion had discovered the relationship between himself and the person to whom the letter was addressed.

"How do you know all that, Dory?" asked Mr. Hawlinshed, trying to calm himself.

"I heard you call him 'Pearl' before I took a hand in the affair," replied Dory candidly. "I don't know that I should ever have thought of the name again if you hadn't given me this letter."

"Then it is very unfortunate that I gave you the letter; but I wished to be sure that it reached him," said Mr. Hawlinshed, very much perplexed at the situation. "You know more than I supposed, and I am very sorry for it. The terrible truth is no longer a secret between my son and myself."

"I ought not to have let on that I knew his name," added Dory, who felt that he had made a mistake.

"Since you knew the fact, I am glad that you spoke. You know that it was my son that attacked me, and who attempted to take the money from me," continued the poor father bitterly.

"But it shall be all the same as though I did not know any thing about it," protested Dory. "After one year or ten you will find that I can keep a secret."

"I am willing to trust you, Dory; and I should be willing, even if I could help myself, and were not entirely in your power," added the unhappy father. "Now you will want to know something about the reason why he attacked me, and tried to get my money from me."

"No, sir: I will not ask any thing about the difficulty. I suppose you and your son could not agree, and I know another case just like it. It is your family affair, and it is none of my business."

"It would take me hours to tell the whole story, and it is too painful to dwell upon. You will keep the secret, Dory?"

"I will never hint that I ever heard your name. I will leave you now, so that no one shall know that I ever saw you, or at least that I ever had any thing to do with you."

"But, Dory, when you tell your mother about the money you have, you will have to explain where you got it. I don't want you to tell any lies about it."

"I shall not give her all the money, and perhaps not any of it," said Dory.

"Not give it to her? I have taken you for a boy who wanted to help his mother; and this view of your character has led me to trust you more than I would if you had not told me your story."

"But I shall use the money for her benefit. I am not going to fool it away. I shall make a business with it which will enable me to help her," replied Dory with enthusiasm.

"What is the business, Dory?"

Dory hesitated. There was a contingency about it, and he was afraid that Mr. Hawlinshed would not approve his plan. He was not altogether clear in regard to it himself, and he did not care to commit himself.

"I should like to keep that as my secret. I am going to help my mother; but I am not sure that I can make the plan work, and I don't want to say any thing about it yet."

"But you will have to explain where you got your money," suggested Mr. Hawlinshed.

"I will promise never to say one word about what happened in the woods. I will give this letter to your son to-morrow morning, and then I will bury the whole thing forever. No one shall ever know where the money came from."

Mr. Hawlinshed had a great many doubts, as well he might have had. But he was in a very trying situation himself. His relations with his son were unpleasant. He had no malice or ill feeling towards Pearl, and all he wanted was to conceal the sad act of the young man.

Dory was very tired; and he could not help gaping, he was so sleepy. He shook hands with his new friend, who said they might never meet again. If he returned to the vicinity of Burlington, he should certainly look him up; and he hoped he should find him an honest, industrious, and prosperous young man. Dory left the room.

He kept one hand in his pocket on the wallet

which contained the treasure that was to open up the brilliant scheme by which he hoped to support his mother and sister. He went out of the hotel without any definite idea of where he intended to go. It was ten o'clock by this time. He was not penniless now, as he had been before. He was rich enough to spend the night, or even a week or a month, at the Witherill House; but the idea of going there, or to any other public house, did not occur to him.

Though he had five dollars for "expenses," he could not think of paying out a dollar, or even half a dollar, for a night's lodging. That would do very well for Mr. Vanderbilt, but not for him. It would be throwing money away. He walked down to the lake. He was not so sleepy as he had been. Stirring himself had waked him up. As he came to the wharf, his brilliant scheme leaped into his head again.

During his stop at Plattsburgh the day before, he had seen a sailboat, which was to be sold at auction with other effects of its deceased owner. He had looked the craft over, and asked a great many questions about her. Though she was twenty-five feet long, and was handsomely fitted up, the knowing ones said she would not bring a hundred dollars at auction.

She could not have cost less than five or six hundred, but she had a bad name. Her late owner had been drowned in consequence of her upsetting. People said it was the fault of the boat. She carried a lee helm, and upset when there was no excuse for her doing so. She had been known to tip over three times, and she was sure to drown whoever bought her.

Dory looked her over very carefully. He had been about all sorts of boats ever since he was a small boy. In fact, he was a natural water-bird, almost as much so as a duck. He was a born mechanic, and his taste not less than his associations had led him to apply his mechanical genius to boats and boating.

The name of the boat was the Goldwing. Dory had examined her the day before, and he "took no stock" in her bad name. He was very sure that any boat would behave badly if rigged and ballasted as the Goldwing was. He wished he owned her, or that he could obtain the use of her for the season. He was confident that he could redeem her reputation.

In connection with this boat had bubbled up his brilliant scheme. If he had her at Burlington, or at several other points on the lake, he could make five dollars a day, if not six or eight, by taking out parties. Such a business was more to his taste, and afforded a better field for his talents, than tending table in the cabin of a steamer.

But it was no use to think of the Goldwing. If five dollars would have bought her, he had not the money to invest in the enterprise. He had no friend upon whom he could call for aid in such a speculation. He might as well think of buying and running one of the large steamers on the lake.

But since dark that evening the whole aspect of his fortunes had changed. He had over a hundred dollars in his pocket, and the Goldwing was to be sold the next day. He did not wish to put all his little fortune into a boat; but he was determined to have the boat, if she was knocked down for a sum within his means.

The Goldwing lay at the wharf. Dory surveyed her as well as he could in the darkness, and then he stepped on board of her. She had been built on purpose for her late owner, on a model somewhat different from her class of boats on the lake; and this created a prejudice against her in the boating fraternity. Dory had seen her frequently under sail, and he was delighted with her.

She was decked over forward, and had a little cabin in this part of the craft. The doors which opened into this apartment were not locked, and Dory went into it. He lighted a match, and discovered a lantern hanging from a deck-beam. He lighted it, and found that the cabin was furnished with two berths, in each of which was a berth-sack. As he looked over this part of the fitting-up of the boat, he gaped again.

He might as well sleep there as in any other place. He had no fear that the ghost of the late owner would disturb him. He arranged the doors so that they could not be opened without waking him, and then lay down in one of the berths. He was going to think over his brilliant scheme; but, before he had done much thinking, he fell asleep.

He did not wake till the swash of the night boat from the south caused the Goldwing to bump against the wharf. It was five o'clock in the morning. He felt in his pocket, and found that his money was safe. He slept another hour after this, and then went on shore. He got his breakfast at a restaurant, and then started to deliver the letter.

He reached his destination in about an hour. He inquired for Pearl Hawlinshed, and found him without any difficulty. He was about twenty-two years old. He did not look like the ferocious being he expected to find in a man who was wicked enough to fire a gun at his father. He was pale, thoughtful in his look, and was rather inclined to melancholy. Dory thought he had enough to think about, and that it was his duty to be melancholy.

Pearl asked him where he got the letter, and Dory said it had been given him by a man in Plattsburgh to bring out to him. He did not wait to answer any questions; and he felt in honor bound not to inquire into any thing relating to Mr. Hawlinshed, father or son.

He returned in season to attend the auction. It was like a funeral party. Dory made the second bid for the boat.

CHAPTER V.

A BOAT WITH A BAD REPUTATION.

PEOPLE looked at the boy as he continued to bid on the Goldwing. The auctioneer asked him some questions touching his ability to pay for the boat if she should be knocked off to him. Dory declared he would pay for the Goldwing on the spot if she was sold to him, and his bid was accepted.

There was only one other bidder, and he looked daggers at Dory every time he increased upon his bid. This man evidently expected to buy the boat for fifteen or twenty dollars, and that there would be no one to bid against him. When the figures reached thirty dollars, the other bidder protested that he was bidding against nothing, for no one supposed that a mere boy could pay for the boat. Until this time Dory had not seen the other person who wanted the Goldwing.

"If he don't pay, Mr. Hawlinshed," said the

auctioneer, "we will put it up again, and then you can get the boat at your own price; for there don't appear to be anybody else that wants the craft."

When Dory heard the name of the other bidder, he turned, and saw that it was Pearl Hawlinshed. He was greatly surprised, and in his confusion he came very near letting the auctioneer knock off the boat to his rival in the contest for the Goldwing. But he put in another bid; and Pearl followed him up sharply until forty dollars was reached, when he declared that he would not give any more for the boat. Then it was knocked off to Dory at forty-two dollars.

Pearl Hawlinshed looked at the purchaser very savagely, as though he had done him an ill turn in bidding for the boat. But there was still a hope that he could not pay for it. Dory went into the cabin of the Goldwing, and counted out the money; for he did not care to show all he had in his wallet. He was out of sight but a moment; for his money was all in ten-dollar bills, except the five which he had changed to pay for his breakfast.

"Here is the money," said Dory, tendering the

amount to the auctioneer. "Please to give me a receipt."

"You have lost the boat, Hawlinshed," said the auctioneer, as he took the money. "If you will come into the steamer office, I will give you a receipt, young man. What is the name?"

"Theodore Dornwood."

"Do you live in Plattsburgh?"

"No, sir: in Burlington."

"Are you buying the boat for yourself?"

"You may make the receipt out to me," replied Dory.

"He is buying her for some other person," said Pearl Hawlinshed. "I should like to know who it is."

The auctioneer did not ask any more questions, but led the way into the steamboat office, where he gave the required receipt. Dory felt that he was now the owner of the Goldwing. If he had owned one of the Champlain steamers, he would not have felt any better. He was anxious to get on board of her, and start her on the way to Burlington. As he went out of the office, he found Pearl Hawlinshed at the door.

"Are you not the boy that brought me a letter

this morning?" asked he, looking at the new owner of the Goldwing with a scowl.

"I carried a letter to you this morning," replied Dory, not particularly pleased with the manner of Pearl.

"Where did you get that letter?" demanded Pearl in a very lordly and overbearing tone.

"A man gave it to me; and I promised to give it to you myself," answered Dory. "That is the whole of it, and nothing more need be said about the matter."

"You said you were buying this boat for another man," continued Pearl.

"I didn't say so. I have not said any thing about who I was buying her for," replied Dory, moving towards the side of the wharf where the Goldwing lay.

"Yes, you did! Don't lie about it," said Pearl in a very offensive way.

"I said nothing of the kind," added Dory.

"Didn't he say he was buying the Goldwing for another man, Mr. Green?" continued Pearl, appealing to the auctioneer.

"No, he did not, Hawlinshed," answered the auctioneer. "I asked him if he was buying the boat for himself, and he said I might make out the receipt to him. That was all that was said about it."

"Well, it is all the same thing: he gave the inference that he was acting for somebody else. I should like to know who you bought her for," persisted Pearl.

"I have bought the boat, and paid for her; and I have nothing more to say about the matter," replied Dory sharply, as he walked towards the boat.

"This is a matter that concerns me, and I want to know about it," added Pearl, following the new owner of the Goldwing to the boat. "You brought me a letter this morning; and now you have bought this boat, when I was the only man in this vicinity that thought of such a thing as buying the Goldwing."

"What has the boat to do with the letter?" asked Dory, who thought it was a little strange that he had come in contact with the son of his new friend in connection with the Goldwing.

"That is what I want to know," answered Pearl gruffly. "You see, I don't believe that a boy like you — for you don't look like the son of a gentleman — came over here from Burlington to buy that boat. If anybody over there had wanted her, he wouldn't have sent a boy over here to buy her for him."

"You can believe any thing you like about it," added Dory, as he stepped into the standing-room of the Goldwing.

"I want to know who gave you that letter," said Pearl, pushing the matter.

"I suppose the man that wrote it gave it to me. You got the letter, and you ought to know more about it than I do."

"I know all about him."

"Then I can't tell you any thing."

"But I want to connect that man with this boat."

"You can connect them if you like. Was there any thing about the Goldwing in the letter?" asked Dory, who was quite as much puzzled as Pearl appeared to be.

"None of your business whether there was or not?" exclaimed Pearl savagely; and the letter was evidently not a pleasant topic to him. "I am not here to answer questions."

"Nor I either; and here we are equal," replied

Dory, as he took the tiller of the sailboat from the forward cuddy, and inserted it in the rudder-head.

"The man that gave you that letter got you to buy this boat for him," said Pearl. "He knew I wanted her, if you did not."

"The man that wrote that letter never said a word to me about this boat, or any other; and I did not buy her for him," replied Dory, startled by the statement of the waspish young man.

Dory was afraid the events of the day might connect him with the elder Mr. Hawlinshed, who had taken the steamer for the south while he was absent in delivering the letter. He had come to the conclusion that Pearl Hawlinshed was a "hard case," as he must be, or he could not have assaulted his father in the woods. There was plainly a quarrel between father and son, and he did not wish to know any thing more about it. All he cared about the matter was to keep the secret inviolate.

"I suppose if you did it you would lie about it," added Pearl.

"You should not judge me by yourself," added Dory quietly.

"Don't give me any of your impudence, or there will be a broken head round here somewhere," snarled Pearl.

Dory did not want a broken head, and he did not want to give the son of his friend a broken head; and he did not want to quarrel with the waspish fellow. He concluded that it would be the wisest policy to say no more, and he went on with his preparations for getting the boat under way. The wind was blowing very fresh from the north-west.

The Goldwing had a bad reputation in Plattsburgh, and he had his doubts about going across the lake in her. He could see the white-caps down Cumberland Bay, and he decided to put a reef in the mainsail. Pearl Hawlinshed was not disposed to leave. He had obtained no satisfaction from the purchaser of the Goldwing, and he evidently believed there was some trickery by which he had been prevented from purchasing the boat at his own price.

"That boat will drown you if you go out in her to-day," said Pearl; and he seemed to realize some satisfaction from the prospect.

"I may not go out in her to-day," replied

Dory, glancing at the white-caps down the bay.

"You were a fool to buy her," added Pearl.

"Am I a greater fool than you would have been if you had bought her?" asked Dory.

"I know just what she wants to make her all right."

"So do I."

Just then a small steamer was seen coming up the bay. She was laboring heavily in the rough waves, and both of them gave their attention to her. She was evidently in the hands of a skipper who did not know how to manage her. The wind had breezed up within an hour, and she had been caught out in the lake. She was within half a mile of the wharf; but Pearl Hawlinshed declared that she would go to the bottom before she reached the pier.

He was quite excited about the steamer, and left the Goldwing to walk down to the end of the wharf, where he could get a better view of the struggling craft. Dory was glad to see him move off. He was as glad to get rid of him as Sindbad was of the Old Man of the Sea. He did not like Pearl: in fact, from what he knew of him, he hated him.

Dory had already hoisted his reefed mainsail. It was shaking and pounding with tremendous energy, as he sat in the standing-room, waiting to decide whether or not he should put out into the lake. But he wanted to get rid of Pearl, and he hoped he should never see him again. While his disagreeable companion was walking down the wharf, he cast off the bow line which held the Goldwing to the pier, and hoisted the jib.

The sails caught the breeze, and the Goldwing darted off from the wharf as though she had been shot from a gun; but she did not exhibit any tendency to go over under her present sail. He ran her outside of the breakwater; and, when he had the boat in a sheltered place, he let go the anchor.

He had got rid of Pearl Hawlinshed, and he was entirely satisfied with himself on this account. He had the Goldwing by himself now, and he immediately proceeded to make another examination of the boat and her furnishings. He got at the ballast, and arranged it to his mind. The fault in the rig he could not correct, but he thought he could overcome the difficulty in this direction in carrying sail.

"Hallo, Dory Dornwood!"

It was the voice of Corny Minkfield; and it came from the little steamer, which had now passed out of danger under the breakwater.

CHAPTER VI.

THE ROBBERY AT THE HOTEL.

PEARL HAWLINSHED found that his prediction in regard to the little steamer was not verified. She did not go to the bottom in spite of her bad management. It was no fault of her skipper that she did not, for he had certainly done his best to sink her. Dory recognized her as a boat that had been kept for all sorts of uses at Burlington.

If Pearl was not satisfied with what had passed between him and the new skipper of the Goldwing, it was too late to do any thing about it now. The boat was off, and he was confident that her skipper had left the wharf to avoid him; for why should he prefer to lie at anchor at the breakwater when her former moorings were so much more convenient?

Pearl Hawlinshed had been a wayward boy. He had worked on his father's farm; he had tended bar at a saloon; he had worked on the steamers on the lake; and now he evidently desired to try his hand at boating. If the Goldwing was worth any thing, she was certainly worth forty dollars; and it is difficult to see why he limited himself to this sum. Perhaps he had no money to buy her, since he had failed to relieve his father of the amount in his possession.

The Goldwing was gone, and there was nothing to keep him on the wharf. He walked up to the Witherill House, where his father had stopped the night before. He was well acquainted there, and he immediately found himself in demand as soon as he entered the office. There appeared to be a considerable excitement about the house.

"You are just the man I want to see, Pearl Hawlinshed," said the landlord, as he entered the office.

"Well, what is wanted of me?" asked Pearl.

"Where has your father gone, Pearl?" asked the landlord, as though he felt a great interest in the question.

"That is more than I know," replied Pearl.

"But he took the boat going south this morning. Don't you know where he has gone?"

"He is going into a lumber speculation in Lawrence County: that's all I know about it. He is going to lose all his money if he can; and I reckon he can," replied Pearl roughly.

"Do you know who the boy was that was with him last night, Pearl? He was a young fellow about fourteen years old. He came into the house with your father, and went up-stairs with him."

"I don't know who he is. What's the matter?" asked the graceless son, wishing to know more before he committed himself.

"A man was robbed of a hundred and fifty dollars in the house last night. He had the room next to your father; and the boy was seen in the hall about ten o'clock in the evening. We thought he might know something about the money," replied the landlord.

"I have no doubt he knows all about it," added Pearl, delighted to connect the purchaser of the Goldwing with a crooked transaction; for he had no doubt that the boy who was with his father had obtained the money with which he bought the boat by stealing it. "This explains the whole matter. It is all as clear as any thing can be now."

"What is clear, Pearl?" asked the landlord.

"The boy who was with my father last nigh has just purchased the Goldwing, poor Lapham' boat; and very likely she will drown the bo before noon, as she did Lapham."

"What has all this to do with the robbery? would rather have given a hundred and fifty dol lars than have the thing happen in my house. Wha has the boat to do with the money lost, Pearl?"

"Why, the boy paid cash for the boat; planke it right down on the nail the moment the boa was knocked off to him," answered Pearl, chuc kling his satisfaction at finding Dory in such scrape.

"Paid cash for the boat, did he? But who i the boy? Does he belong in Plattsburgh?" aske the landlord, beginning to see the relation of th boat to the money.

"The boy says his name is Theodore Dorn wood, and that he lives in Burlington."

"Dornwood!" exclaimed the landlord. "Tha was the name of the pilot that wrecked the A Sable last night."

"Wrecked the Au Sable?" repeated Pea curiously.

"Haven't you heard the news?"

"I haven't heard any such news as that. Is she really wrecked? I used to work on that boat," added Pearl, opening his eyes very wide.

"Where have you been all the morning? It has got to be an old story by this time. The Au Sable was run on shore, and sunk. No one was lost; but several were injured,—how many, I don't know."

"But how came she ashore? It wasn't even foggy last night," said Pearl.

"That's the mystery. The boat ran on to a point of rocks. The report thinks the pilot in charge was trying to run the boat over the land. His name was Dornwood; and he must have been either drunk or asleep, or both. But all this is neither here nor there. What about this boy? He may be the son of this pilot for aught we know."

"I don't know any Dornwood. He was not a pilot in her when I was on the Au Sable."

"How do you know that the boy who was with your father bought the Goldwing, Pearl?" inquired the landlord, who had told his news and lost his interest in it till another uninformed person came along. "I don't want to accuse any person of robbing my house without the means of proving the charge."

"Oh, it's all straight, you may depend upon it!" replied Pearl. "I thought the boy looked like a young rascal, and now I know that he stole the money. Of course it is no sale, so far as the boat is concerned. How is that?" asked Pearl, who seemed to realize for the first time, that, if the money paid for the Goldwing was stolen, it would have to be returned to the rightful owner.

"I should say it would be no trade under the circumstances. But you don't tell me how you know it was this boy that was with your father last night in my house," said the landlord impatiently.

"I don't know that he was in your house with my father. He was with my father last night, for he told me so. He brought me a letter from my father this morning. When we were bidding on the Goldwing, I found it was the same boy. That's how I know it; and there is no mistake about it," added Pearl.

"It looks as though there might be something in it. At any rate we will have the thing looked into. Where is the boy now? What has become of him?"

"The last I saw of him he was in the Goldwing, at anchor off the breakwater, on the outside. I have no doubt he is going to Burlington in the boat as soon as the weather is fit for him to sail."

"Perhaps he has gone by this time," suggested the landlord.

"I don't believe he has. It is blowing heavy out on the lake; and the boy knows what sort of a boat the Goldwing is, for I warned him that she would drown him."

"There seems to be no doubt that the boy is the same one that went to your father's room last night, though that don't prove that he robbed the room of one of my guests. I should like to see the boy, and have him explain what he has been about," added the landlord.

"We will have him arrested if he can't tell a straight story," said Pearl. "If you authorize me to do it, I will bring the boy up here; but I may have to get a steamer to chase him, and there will be some expense about it."

"I will pay any reasonable expense," replied

the landlord. "You are not an officer, and of course you can't arrest him."

"But I will bring him up here, whether I am an officer or not," continued Pearl. "I am as much interested in getting him back as you are."

"How is that?"

"I wanted to buy the Goldwing; and I expected to get her for about twenty dollars, though her sails cost more than that. The young rascal tricked me out of her. If he stole the money, it is no trade, and the boat will have to be put up again."

The landlord was satisfied that Pearl would bring the boy to the hotel if it were possible. Pearl was very sure that he would do it. Without knowing any thing particular about the Burlington boy, he had taken an intense dislike to him; but he had no suspicion that he was the person who had interfered with his operations in the woods the night before. He hastened down to the wharf, where he found the little steamer that he had seen struggling with the big waves in the lower bay.

"You have had a rough time of it," said Pearl to a man he found on the deck of the boat.

"Rather rough; but we came through all right," replied the man.

"What boat is this?" inquired the thief-taker, as he already regarded himself.

"This is the Missisquoi. A man in Plattsburgh bought her, and I came to fetch her over; but he won't be here till to-morrow night," replied the temporary skipper. "I fetched over a lot of boys from Burlington, and they made things lively on the way."

"Do you know a boy in Burlington by the name of Theodore Dornwood?" asked Pearl.

"Well, I guess I do. Everybody that has any thing to do with boats in Burlington knows all about him. He is a little wild, but he is as smart as a steel trap," replied Captain Vesey, as he was called by courtesy.

"Is he an honest boy?" asked Pearl, as though that were a matter of the utmost consequence to him.

"I guess he is. He is worth two of his father, who was the pilot on duty on board of the Au Sable last night, and tried to take the boat across a p'int of land. He didn't make out, and I guess it will be a bad job for him."

"Where are the boys you brought over?" inquired Pearl, looking about the boat for them.

"You see, they came over here on a lark, and will have to get back the best way they can. We found Dory in a sailboat, anchored off the breakwater. The boys wanted me to put them aboard of her, and I did. Dory says he is going to sail the boat to Burlington, and the rest of the boys are going with him. They are the wildest set of boys on the lake."

"I suppose you don't object to earning five dollars with this boat before you deliver her to her owner?" suggested Pearl in an indifferent sort of way.

"I guess not," said Captain Vesey, with a broad grin on his face. "I never object to making five dollars, or one dollar, for that matter."

"I want to see Dory Dornwood on some particular business; and, if you will put me on board of his boat, I will give you five dollars," said Pearl in an insinuating tone.

Captain Vesey was ready to do it.

CHAPTER VII.

THE MAN THAT LOOKED THROUGH THE KEY-HOLE.

PEARL HAWLINSHED had not looked to see if the Goldwing was where he had last seen her, outside of the breakwater. The water was unusually low on the lake; and, though he saw the topmasts of several boats beyond the breakwater, he was unable to determine whether or not any of them belonged to the Goldwing. Captain Vesey had seen no boat go out, and Pearl concluded that she was still at anchor.

Pearl made his trade with the acting skipper of the little steamer, which was hardly more than a steam-launch. Mr. Button the engineer, who was to remain in the employ of the new owner, was wiping the water off the machinery. He was called, and informed of the arrangement with Pearl. To the astonishment of both, he refused to move the Missisquoi from the wharf.

"I reckon the boat is in my care until she is delivered to the new owner," argued Captain Vesey.

"It don't make any difference to me whose care she is in. I won't go out with a man who don't know any more about handling a boat than you do, Captain Vesey," replied Mr. Button warmly. "It was only by a miracle that we got over here at all. I expected to go to the bottom every minute of the time until we got inside of the breakwater."

"I reckon I know how to handle a steamboat as well as the next man," returned Captain Vesey indignantly.

"That depends upon how much the next man knows about a tug-boat. If the next man don't know any more about it than you do, I don't want to run the engine for him."

Pearl could not help being on the engineer's side of the controversy. He and Dory had agreed that the captain of the Missisquoi did not understand his business. But Pearl Hawlinshed believed that he knew all about a steamer, and all about the lake. He considered himself competent to command one of the large steamers.

"I am going with you, Mr. Button, and it will be five dollars in your pocket, as well as the captain's," interposed Pearl, who was disposed to be liberal with the landlord's money.

"My life is worth something to me; or at any rate it is to my family," replied Mr. Button doubtfully. "Do you know about handling such a boat as this?"

"I know all about it: I used to sail in the Au Sable," replied Pearl confidently.

Mr. Button was doubtless a good engineer, but he was not a very shrewd man. If he had been, he would have asked in what capacity the applicant for the use of the Missisquoi served on board of the Au Sable. Possibly Pearl would have evaded the question, or lied about the matter, for he had simply been a waiter in the cabin for a few weeks. But Pearl thought he knew all about a steamer, and all about the navigation of the lake.

"If you are a steamboat man I have no objection to taking the boat out," added the engineer. "It is a very rough day on the lake, and one has to know something about handling a boat in such big waves."

"But I am the captain of this boat, and I

reckon I don't want any boss over me," interposed Captain Vesey at this point.

"We shall have no trouble," added Pearl, as he walked aft with the captain. "I shall not meddle with your management of the boat. I only said what I did to quiet the engineer."

But the boat had to take in a supply of fuel, for which Pearl promised to pay out of the landlord's pocket. She could not leave for a couple of hours. Pearl wanted to go back to the hotel, and attend to some matters in connection with his mission which he had forgotten.

"I am to pay you five dollars, and the engineer five dollars, when you put me on board of the Goldwing," said Pearl, as he was about to leave the boat. "Is that the trade?"

"That's it," replied the engineer; and so answered the captain.

Pearl walked up the pier, and then went down the railroad till he could see outside of the breakwater. He found the Goldwing lay at anchor in the place she had chosen at first. Ten dollars would be a good sum to pay if the Missisquoi was obliged to take him only out to the breakwater. But, the sooner he brought Dory on shore, the sooner the Goldwing would be put up at auction again.

He walked to the Witherill House, and informed the landlord of what he had done, and declared that the boy who had stolen the money should be handed over to him in a couple of hours. The hotel-keeper did not object to the expense; but he wished his representative to be careful how he managed the business, for it was by no means certain that the boy had taken the money.

"I am as certain of it as I am of my own existence," replied Pearl warmly. "I have found out something about the boy since I was here. He has the reputation of being wild, and no one sent him over here to buy a boat. And a fellow like him don't have forty or fifty dollars to invest in boats."

"All that may be; but you can be careful just as well as not," added the landlord.

"He is nothing but a young cub, and has no friends, so that nothing will come of it if he shouldn't happen to be the thief."

"If he has no one to defend him, so much the more reason why he should be fairly dealt with," replied the hotel-keeper,—a sentiment with which Pearl Hawlinshed had no sympathy. "I have seen Moody since you went out, and he says a man was looking into the keyhole of the room next to his about ten o'clock last evening. That was your father's room. Have you any idea who that man was, Hawlinshed?"

"I haven't the least idea in the world," answered Pearl; and possibly the landlord did not notice his confusion when he replied, "Very likely it was this same boy."

"It wasn't a boy, but a man: I asked Moody particularly about this matter."

"I don't know any thing about the matter at all," protested Pearl. "If the man that lost the money saw any thing of this kind, why didn't he tell of it before?"

"I asked him this question, and he says he did not think of it before. The fact of it is, that Moody had been drinking, though he sticks to it that he wasn't drunk. He went into his room at about ten o'clock, and put the money into his trunk, for he was afraid he might lose it. He saw the man looking in at the keyhole of your father's room when he went into his own to put the money in a safe place. He heard voices in the next room when he opened his trunk. The boy was with your father at that time very likely."

"If the man had been drinking, it is not probable that he knows much about the boy or the man," added Pearl.

"He had not got very tipsy, or he would not have thought to look out for his money. But bring the boy up, if you can get him without violence or outrage. If he explains where he got the money to buy the boat, that is the end of the matter so far as he is concerned. In my opinion the man who was looking in at the keyhole of your father's room is more likely to be the thief than the boy."

"Where did the boy get forty-two dollars to pay for the boat, then?" demanded Pearl.

"I give it up," laughed the landlord. "But we are likely to know something more about the case before dinner-time. I called in Peppers, who used to be a detective in New York City; and he is at work on the case now."

"What did you do that for?" demanded Pearl, who did not seem to relish the information.

"You set me at work on the case; and now you have called in another person to attend to it, after I have engaged a steamer."

"All I asked you to do was to bring the boy in to be questioned. Peppers won't interfere with any thing that you may do," replied the landlord, not a little surprised at the objection of Pearl.

"What is Peppers doing?" asked Pearl uneasily.

"I don't know what he is doing: at least, I don't know much about it, and he told me not to tell what I did know."

"But you can tell me, for I am at work on the case," said Pearl in a coaxing tone.

"No: I won't tell you any thing. You won't interfere with each other; and it is best for each of you to work on his own hook," replied the hotel-keeper, as he turned to attend to a guest who wished to speak to him.

Pearl saw that it was useless to press the matter any farther; and he was evidently very much disturbed about the turn the investigation had taken during his absence. He was particularly anxious to know what the detective was about, but he was unable to obtain any information from any person. He returned to the steamboat wharf. When he came in sight of the breakwater, he was not a little startled to see the Goldwing dart out from behind the structure, with only a small jib and a reefed mainsail.

He was startled; because not more than an hour had elapsed since he left the Missisquoi, and he expected it would be another hour before she would be ready to go in pursuit of the Goldwing. The latter could sail like the wind if she would only keep right side up, and she would get a long start of the steamer. Besides, Pearl did not like the looks of the big waves on the lake any better than Mr. Button had; and he was not altogether sure that he could manage her any better than Captain Vesey had done.

The Goldwing was running from the end of the breakwater over towards the main shore, and it was possible that Dory intended to make a landing at Plattsburgh. But it was not more than a quarter of a mile from the breakwater to the shore, and he could soon tell what she intended to do. He hastened down the railroad to settle this point. In the furious breeze that was blowing, the Goldwing seemed to leap over the water. If she intended to go up to the wharf from which she had started, she would have to tack in a moment.

Pearl ran with all his might; for it occurred to him that if he could induce Dory to come on shore and go up to the hotel with him, he might save the ten dollars he had agreed to give the captain and engineer, and contrive some way to have it stick in his own pocket. The Goldwing ran within a hundred feet of the shore, and Pearl got behind a car on a side track to ascertain what she intended to do.

Gradually her main sheet was let off, and the Goldwing was headed to the southward. This settled the matter. The boat was not going back to the wharf. Her skipper had evidently run her over in that direction in order to get her under the lee of the shore, where she would not get the full force of the wind.

"Hallo! on board of the Goldwing!" shouted Pearl, as he ran to the water's edge, yelling as loud as he could.

"On shore!" replied Dory, "what do you want?"

"You are wanted at the hotel," replied Pearl.

Dory discovered by this time who it was that hailed him; and he took no further notice of Pearl, who hastened to the wharf.

CHAPTER VIII.

THE COLCHESTER CLUB CHANGES ITS NAME.

"WHAT in the world are you doing over here, fellows?" asked Dory Dornwood, as the four passengers of the Missisquoi tumbled in over the stern of the Goldwing.

"And what under the breezes of Lake Champlain are you doing in this boat?" shouted Thad Glovering, who was the first to get a footing in the standing-room of the Goldwing.

"What boat is it?" asked Nat Long in a blustering manner.

"What are you going to do with her, Dory?" demanded Dick Short.

"Can't you take us over to Burlington in her?" queried Corny Minkfield.

"How many questions do you think I can answer at once, fellows?" replied Dory. "I am going over to Burlington as soon as the weather is fit; and you can go with me if you like."

"All right, Dory! Hurrah for Dory Dornwood! You are all right, and so are we: only we are half starved, for we haven't had any breakfast this morning," said Thad Glovering.

It must be confessed that the party that arrived in the Missisquoi were not very promising-looking boys. They had a wild, harum-scarum appearance and manner, which fully justified the description Captain Vesey had given of them. In a word, they were evidently wild boys; and in this respect they did not differ much from Dory himself.

They are the boat-builders whose exploits and achievements are to be recorded, and they may as well be introduced at this as at any other time. Thad Glovering was an orphan, who lived with his uncle. As this relative had several children of his own, the added one was a burden to him, for he had but small wages. Thad declared that he was willing to work; but up to this time nothing had been found for him to do. The worst that could be said of him was that he was wild.

Nat Long's father was a deck-hand on a steamer; and, as he was away most of the time, Nat

"THE FOUR PASSENGERS TUMBLED IN OVER THE STERN OF THE GOLDWING." PAGE 87.

was permitted to have his own way. His mother was dead; and his older sister, who had the care of the family, found herself unable to control him. He was not a confirmed bad boy, and had worked for a year in one place, and done very well. A change in the business had thrown him out of work, and he had been unable to find another situation. Idleness led him into mischief; and, without some kind of control, it was only a question of time when he got into the hands of the law for some crime.

Dick Short and Corny Minkfield were the sons of widows, both of whom had some property. Their mothers were able to support them without work; but work was the one thing they needed, whether it was with the head or the hands.

These five boys lived near together, and they had been cronies from their earliest school-days. Two of them were usually well dressed; and the others were somewhat ragged, and considerably patched, showing the efforts of their protectors to keep them decent. They had all been to school up to the present time, and now it was vacation; and the next thing to be decided by their friends was what should be done with them. Dick and Corny were to go to the high school; but the others must go to work, and earn their own living,—do something for the support of their parents.

Dory had gone to work before the school closed for the summer, and all the boys talked as though they intended to do something. But they did not feel like going to work in vacation time. They had always had great larks on the lake when school did not keep, and they were not disposed to dispense with the good time the present year.

It could not be said that one of these boys was really bad. But they kept all kinds of company; and, in the absence of any strong controlling force, they were in great danger of becoming "hard boys." Sometimes they assisted about the steamers and other vessels; and, by making themselves useful, they obtained the privilege of sailing on the lake. Their associations were not always of the best character. They were all "smart boys;" and wise and steady people who knew them wished they might be put to some useful labor, or be subjected to some salutary control. Mrs. Short and Mrs. Minkfield had both been warned of the peril of their sons; and both had considered the means of redeeming them from the bad company into which their habits threw them. But they had not done any thing beyond reasoning with the boys, who always promised to mend their ways.

Assisted by his four cronies, Dory Dornwood had built a sort of bateau, a flat-bottomed craft, in which they used to row about the lake near the shore. It was a rude boat; for the young boat-builders had few tools, and very inferior lumber for the construction of the bateau. But it would carry them all, and Dory was the captain of the craft. She was called the Colchester; and the boys formed a club for aquatic sports, to which they gave the name of the boat.

Doubtless the Colchester Club gave a great deal of satisfaction to its members. Unfortunately the Colchester broke adrift in a September squall, and went to pieces on Colchester Reef, as reported by the light-keeper. No other boat could be obtained; but the members all said that as soon as they got to work they should give a portion of their earnings for the purchase of a suitable craft for the association. Up to this time they had not gone to work, and the successor of the Colchester did not appear.

Dory proceeded to answer the questions of his fellow-members of the Colchester Club. The boat in which they found him belonged to him; and this was the most astounding statement he made in the course of the interview. They opened their eyes, and stared at Captain Dory, as they called him, in silent wonder. Then they looked the boat over with renewed interest, and seemed to be unable to believe the statement of their companion.

"The Colchester Club shall have the use of her when I am on board," added Dory magnanimously.

"That's handsome; and we shall have the biggest kind of times," added Thad Glovering. "I'll tell you what we'll do, fellows. We will change the name of the club, and call it after this boat. What is her name, Dory?"

"You will find it on the stern, and also on the bowsprit," replied the skipper of the Goldwing. "It isn't a bad name either."

Two of the members of the club looked over

the stern, and two others rushed to the bow. The name was of the utmost consequence, and Dory thought it was better for them to read it for themselves than for him to tell it. Besides, there was a good deal of style in the way the name was put on in the three places.

"Goldwing!" shouted Corny Minkfield, who was the first to read the name on the stern. "And there is a gold wing under it."

"Goldwing!" repeated Dick Short, as he read the name on the heel of the bowsprit. "And there is a gold wing here too."

"Isn't that a splendid name for a boat! Goldwing!" exclaimed Nat Long. "I don't think you could find any thing better than that if you should study for a month."

"Or any thing better for a club," added Thad Glovering. "The Goldwing Club! How do you think that sounds, fellows?"

"I don't believe any thing could sound any better," added Dick Short. "But we haven't looked the boat over yet."

All hands proceeded to attend to this duty at once. The Colchester had been a rough, flat-bottomed craft, with neither shape nor comeliness about her. Whatever first-class sailboats the members of the club had seen had been only at a distance; and consequently their ideal of beauty, symmetry, comfort, and convenience in a boat was not very high. The Goldwing was perfection itself to them, though it might not have been to more experienced observers. They were ecstatic in their praises of the Goldwing, and did not believe there was a finer sailboat on the lake than she was.

"You don't mean to say that you own this craft, Dory Dornwood!" said Thad when the party had exhausted their vocabulary of fine words applicable to a beautiful sailboat.

"I have said it once, and I will say it again if it will do any good," replied Dory. "The Goldwing is mine, and she don't belong to anybody else. You can go the last cent you've got on that."

"Get out, Dory!" exclaimed Dick Short, punching the skipper in the ribs. "You are selling us too cheap, Dory."

"I'm not selling you at all!" protested Dory. "I wouldn't take twenty-five cents apiece for you, though that would make a dollar."

"You can't expect us to believe that you own such a magnificent boat as this, Dory, unless you tell us where you got her," said Corny Minkfield very seriously.

"I can expect it, and I do expect it," added Dory, taking the auctioneer's receipt from his pocket. "I shall prove to you that she is mine, and without saying another word."

Dory handed the receipt to Corny, and said nothing more. The sceptic read the paper out loud, and of course that settled the question. There was no room for a doubt after the reading of the receipt.

"Forty-two dollars!" exclaimed Corny, as he handed the receipt back to the skipper. "Judging by the cost of the Letitia, she ought to be worth four or five hundred dollars."

"Forty-two dollars is nothing for a boat like this," added Dick Short, whose mother was worth money, and therefore he had less respect for forty-two dollars than most of the other members.

"But where did you get the forty-two dollars?" asked Thad, who had hardly ever possessed even half a dime at one time.

"Haven't I proved that the Goldwing is mine?"

demanded Dory rather warmly; for he did not want his fellow-members of the Goldwing Club skirmishing adout in the region of the great secret of his lifetime. "All I have to say about it is, that I came honestly by the money, and I don't want any more questions asked."

Dory Dornwood, though he was rather wild, scorned to invent a lie to explain where the money came from, as perhaps some of his companions might have done under similar circumstances.

The other members of the Goldwing Club looked at one another; and Nat Long winked at Corny Minkfield, as much as to say "There is a cat in the meal somewhere." After the imperative warning from the skipper that nothing more was to be said about the forty-two dollars, no more questions were asked; but it was evident that the members all kept up a tremendous thinking on the subject. But even this matter became stale in a few minutes in the excitement of the hour.

"Forty-two dollars is dirt cheap for a boat like the Goldwing," said Dory, breaking the silence. "I have no doubt she cost four or five hundred dollars; but I ought to tell you that she has a bad name."

"A bad name! The Goldwing?" exclaimed Thad; and all of the party seemed to think it quite impossible that such a splendid boat as the Goldwing could have any thing but a first-class reputation.

"She drowned the man that owned her. She upset, and then went to the bottom. Now, if any of you want to go on shore, you can."

The members of the Goldwing Club looked aghast at one another.

CHAPTER IX.

A WEATHER HELM AND A LEE HELM.

"IS the Goldwing in the habit of upsetting? Does she make a regular thing of it?" asked Thad Glovering.

"I have heard of her doing it twice before; though I believe she never drowned any one but her owner," replied Dory candidly and seriously. "But I don't want any fellow to sail in her that don't want to."

"We can stand it as well as you can, Dory," added Corny Minkfield. "I suppose she would drown you as easily as she would any of the rest of us."

"There is nothing to make any of us stand it if we don't want to," continued Dory. "I have told you the worst of it, and there isn't any law to make any of you sail in the Goldwing."

"But we want to sail in her; and this is the Goldwing Club now. But we don't want to be drowned," said Thad. "I think my uncle would like to get rid of me, but I don't believe he would want to have me drowned."

"I don't want to be drowned any more than you do, and I know my mother wouldn't want any such thing to happen to me. Of course I wouldn't go out in the Goldwing if I thought she was going to spill me into the lake," added Dory. "I have told you the worst of it, and now you can go ashore at Plattsburgh if you want to."

"I am willing to take my chances if you are, Dory," replied Thad with some hesitation. "It is blowing a young hurricane to-day, and you said you should not go till the weather was fit."

"I am not going to drown myself or you either, if I can help it, fellows," Dory proceeded. "I heard about the Goldwing the last time I was up here. I asked all about the drowning of the man that owned her, and a boatman who saw the whole of it told me all about it."

"How long ago was it that the man was drowned?" asked Nat Long.

"It was about three weeks ago. The boat lay on the bottom a week before they raised her," replied Dory.

"Was it blowing hard when he was drowned?" inquired Corny.

"No: it was just a good sailing-breeze. I think I know what the matter was with the boat. I believe I can make her all right, if I have not already done it; for I have been at work on her this morning."

"What was the trouble with her?" asked Thad, who considered the skipper competent to put any thing to rights about a boat.

"She was ballasted so that she carried a lee helm," answered Dory, as solemnly as though he settled the fate of a nation by his words.

"Carried a lee helm!" exclaimed Dick Short. "Is that what the matter was?"

"Carried a lee helm!" repeated Thad. "That was bad!"

"Carried a lee helm! If it was bad for her, she ought to have left her lee helm on shore."

"What did she carry it for?" asked Nat Long.

"She carried it because she couldn't leave it behind," replied Dory. "It is a bad habit, such as some men carry with them through life, for the reason that they can't get rid of it."

"I say, Dory, what is a lee helm?" asked Thad. "You know that we don't know any thing more about sailing a boat than we do about making a watch."

"You used to sail Mr. Jones's boat: but we never went with you then, Dory; and we never had any chance to learn how to sail a boat," added Corny. "I have no more idea what a lee helm is than I have what the man in the moon had for dinner to-day."

"That's what's the matter with all of us," added Thad, laughing.

"I didn't mean to bother you, fellows; but that is just what ailed the Goldwing, and she had it bad. But any boat would have behaved in the same way if she was not properly trimmed. I don't think Mr. Lapham — that's the man that owned the Goldwing, and was drowned; I couldn't think of his name before — understood a boat very well. Look here, fellows!"

Dory Dornwood pointed to a mast-hole in the deck, which had been stopped. The foremast had been moved nearly two feet aft of the place where it had been stepped by the builder.

"The boatman told me that Mr. Lapham had

changed the place of the foremast, so that he could make room for a locker in the head. If she had a bigger jib, it would be all right. The ballast was badly stowed, and that is what made her carry a lee helm."

"Now we know all about what did it, but we don't know what a lee helm is," added Thad, laughing. "I wish you would tell us what the thing is before you say any thing else."

"A boat ought to carry a weather helm, though not too much of it," replied Dory, knitting his brow as though he was struggling with a big idea, though he was only thinking how he should make his companions understand him.

The other members of the Goldwing Club could pull an oar or handle a paddle; and that was really all they knew about boating, though they were very ambitious to learn.

"I believe that. A boat ought to carry a weather helm. I think the legislature ought to make a law that a boat should carry a weather helm, and make it a state-prison offence to carry a lee helm, which is very bad," said Corny Minkfield.

"If you are going to do all the talking, I haven't any thing more to say," replied Dory with dignity.

"Don't get mad, Dory. We don't know what a weather helm is any better than we do what a lee helm is," added Corny, as an apology for the interruption.

"I was going to tell you what a weather helm is; for, when you know what one is, you will understand the other: but you keep putting your oars in, fellows, so that I don't get a chance."

"We won't say another word until we know what a weather helm is, and what a lee helm is," said Thad. "Dry up, fellows! not another word."

"A boat ought to carry a weather helm," Dory began again; and then he paused to give his companions a chance to interrupt him.

Corny was just going to remind him that he had said this before, when Thad put his finger on his lips, and the remark was suppressed. Dory looked at them all, and found that they intended to "give him the floor;" and then he proceeded with his explanation.

"The wind don't always blow just the same," Dory proceeded; and Corny could hardly help making a comment on this sage remark. "I don't mean on different days, but within the same hour. In other words, the wind don't come steady. To-day it comes down in heavy flaws. You can see the effect of the puffs on the top of the water. A vessel keeps tipping a little in almost any breeze."

The members of the Goldwing Club nodded all around to indicate that they understood the matter so far.

"When a flaw or puff comes," Dory continued, "it changes the course of the boat. The helm has to be shifted to meet this change. Almost always the tiller has to be carried to the weather side of the boat. Do you know which the weather side of the boat is, fellows?" asked the expounder of nautical matters.

"It is the side the weather is on, of course," replied Corny.

"It is the side from which the wind comes," added Thad, who thought it was not quite fair to make fun of the remarks of the skipper when he was doing his best to have them understand the difficulty with the Goldwing.

"And what do you call the other side?" asked Dory.

"The lee side, I think," answered Thad.

"Right, Thad; and Corny was not so far out

of the way as he meant to be, for to a sailor the wind is about all there is of the weather. When a flaw comes, and you have to carry the tiller to the weather side of the boat to keep her on her course, that is a weather helm," Dory proceeded.

"I see it!" exclaimed Nat Long, as though he had made a great discovery.

"I don't believe you do, Nat," interposed the skipper. "Suppose you don't carry the tiller to the weather side, what will happen then?"

"I don't know that any thing will happen," answered Nat, rather abashed at his own ignorance.

"That's the point of all that has been said," added Dory.

"Well, what will happen? Will she tip over?" asked Nat.

"That is the very thing she won't do; and that's the reason why a boat ought to carry a weather helm, so that she won't tip over if the helmsman don't happen to have his eyes wide open tight. If you don't put the helm to the weather side, the head of the boat will come up to the wind. As she comes up into the wind, it spills the sail."

"Spills the sail!" exclaimed Corny, who could hold in no longer. "I have heard of spilling the milk, but not of spilling a sail."

"It means to spill the wind out of the sail," added Dory. "In other words, it takes the wind out of the sail, and it don't press against the sail any longer. And, if the wind don't press against the sail, of course it won't tip the boat over."

"That's plain enough. I understand that first-rate," said Thad. "If a puff brings the boat up into the wind, then the wind don't bear hard on the sail, and it won't upset the boat."

"Now let us see how it works when a boat carries a lee helm. Instead of coming up into the wind when a flaw strikes the sail, some boats go the other way. The flaw crowds them off from the wind. The more she falls off, the harder the wind presses against the sail. If the puff throws the head of the boat far enough from the wind, it will blow square against it; and, if there is enough of it, it will upset any boat. Then, if you have to put the helm away from the wind in order to keep the course, that's a lee helm; and it's a dangerous thing in any boat, though it can generally be easily corrected if the skipper understands the matter."

"I see it," said Thad. "I suppose the owner of this boat did not understand it."

"They say he was obstinate about it, and would not take the advice of those who did understand the matter," added Dory. "I have shifted the ballast; and I think the Goldwing will work all right now, though I wish the foremast was in the old hole."

The members of the club declared that they understood the matter perfectly. They were willing to return to Burlington in the Goldwing if it could be shown that she carried a weather helm. When the skipper had finished his explanation, he went forward, and took another look at the hole which had been stopped. He found a shingling hatchet in the cuddy, and with this he attempted to drive out the filling of the mast-hole. After a deal of pounding, he succeeded in the attempt.

He lost no time in demolishing the locker in the head which Mr. Lapham had fitted there. For an hour he worked very diligently, assisted by all the other members of the club; and the foremast was transferred to the hole the builder had intended it should occupy. The stays were adjusted again with the greatest care on the part of the skipper, and made strong enough for the heavy weather that prevailed on the lake.

"Isn't there any thing to eat on board, Dory?" asked Thad. "We are almost starved."

There was not a morsel of food on board, but Dory said he would go over to the town if he could.

CHAPTER X.

THE MISSISQUOI IN PURSUIT.

OF course Dory Dornwood had no suspicion of what had transpired on shore since he departed in the Goldwing. The hunger of the other members of the club reminded him that he might make a long passage to Burlington, or that he might be compelled to lie at anchor for a whole day before it was safe to cross the lake in the present state of the weather. He might be hungry himself as well as his companions, and he had not thought to lay in a stock of provisions for the voyage.

For this reason he was all the more willing to land at Plattsburgh. He hoisted the reefed mainsail again, and directed a couple of the party to get up the anchor. The Goldwing darted off at a furious rate, as she had before, when the fresh breeze filled her sails. She took the wind on her quarter at first; but Dory soon braced her up as she rounded the southerly beacon at the end of the breakwater, and headed the boat for the main shore.

"How does she work now, Dory?" asked Thad when the boat was on her course. "Does she carry a lee helm?"

"Not at all. It takes all my strength to keep her from luffing up," replied the skipper.

"There's another new word," added Corny Minkfield. "What in the world does 'luffing up' mean?"

"'To luff' is to come into the wind. I mean by that, to turn the head of the boat in the direction from which the wind comes," replied Dory. "But what she does under her present sail don't settle the question. I took the bonnet off the jib before I left the wharf this morning."

"The bonnet!" shouted Corny. "Does the boat wear a bonnet?"

"Of course she does. You never made the mistake of putting a boat in the masculine gender. You always say 'she' in speaking of a boat; and of course she wears a bonnet when she goes out."

"But when the weather is bad you take the bonnet off; and that is not the way the ladies do" suggested Thad.

"In rough weather the bonnet makes it all the rougher," added Dory. "The bonnet is a continuation of the jib, laced to the lower part of the sail. Taking off the bonnet amounts to the same thing as reefing the sail."

"Reefing the sail is taking in a part of the sheet by tying it up in a fold," said Nat Long, looking very wise.

"Not much!" answered the skipper.

"That's what my father told me; and he is a deck-hand on board of the Champlain," persisted Nat.

"I don't believe he said any thing of the kind, Nat. Taking up a part of the sheet by tying it into a fold would be a queer operation. Do you run away with the idea that the jib is a sheet?"

"I don't run away with the idea; but of course a sail is a sheet."

"Not at all. This is a sheet," answered Dory, raising the main sheet, the end of which he held in his left hand, while he steered with his right.

"How can that be a sheet when it is a rope?" demanded Nat incredulously.

"You are thinking of the sheets between which you sleep. In a boat all sheets are ropes. This is the main sheet, because it is fastened to the main boom, — the stick at the lower part of the sail. This is the jib sheet," continued Dory, indicating the rope attached to the lower part of the jib, which led aft into the standing-room, where the helmsman could haul it in or let it off as occasion required.

"There is a man hailing us from the shore," said Thad, as Pearl Hawlinshed called to Dory from the railroad.

"I don't want to see that man," said Dory, recognizing the voice of the disagreeable man from whom he had fled when he left the wharf.

"Do you know him?" asked Thad.

"I never saw him until this morning. He bid against me for this boat, and he is mad because he didn't get it," replied the skipper. "I think he means to do me mischief if he can, and he can't if I keep out of his way."

He could not answer any questions without endangering his great secret. He was on the point of tacking when he heard the call. To go up to the wharf would be to fall into the company of Pearl, and he decided not to do it. Instead of coming about, he let off the sheets, and headed the Goldwing to the southward.

"You are going the wrong way, Dory," said Thad.

"I don't care about going on shore at Plattsburgh again, fellows; but we will get something to eat at Port Jackson," replied Dory, without explaining his reason for not wishing to land at the town.

"But we shall starve to death before you get there," protested Corny. "We have not had a mouthful of any thing to eat to-day. Captain Vesey said we might go with him if we would be on board at five o'clock in the morning, and we had no chance to get any breakfast."

"I am sorry I can't do any thing for you just now; but it is only six miles to Port Jackson, and I think we shall be there in about an hour," replied Dory. "I think the fellow that hailed me is wicked enough to get this boat away from me if he can; and I don't care about meeting him again."

The members of the Goldwing Club settled down in the most comfortable places they could find. A couple of them took possession of the berths in the cuddy, and two others stretched themselves on the seats in the standing-room.

They were not so wild as Captain Vesey had reported them to be on the passage from Burlington. They were faint and hungry; for it was now nearly noon, and the voyagers in the Missisquoi had fasted the greater part of twenty-four hours.

The Goldwing was under the lee of the land, where there was no sea; but the wind came in very sharp puffs, as the openings in the shore exposed the boat to the unsteady blast. But she carried so little sail that she went along very easily, and showed no more tendency to upset than any well-built boat would in such puffy weather. The party on board saw nothing in her behavior to warrant the bad reputation she had established.

Three miles brought the boat to Bluff Point; and the shore was so elevated here, that the skipper stood farther out into the lake so that he might not lose the wind. The Goldwing behaved so well, that Dory was beginning to have a great deal of confidence in her, so that he did not hesitate to venture farther from the shore.

The schooner appeared to be making about six miles an hour. Passing between Valcour's Island and the main land, the Goldwing arrived at

Port Jackson inside of an hour; but, before the boat entered the little bay on which the port is situated, the boys had another sensation. Dory had hardly thought of looking astern in the run of the Goldwing down from Plattsburgh.

"There's a steamer coming down the same way we did," said Dick Short, as he rose from his place on the seat, just as the schooner was going into the port. "It looks just like the Missisquoi."

"It is the Missisquoi," added Thad, after he had surveyed the boat.

"It certainly looks like her," said Dory, who was trying to make out what this appearance meant.

His companions had told him the destination of the Missisquoi; and he was satisfied that she could have no business in this part of the lake, as she was to be used in towing lumber in the north. He had seen the little steamer go up to the wharf where the Goldwing lay. He could not get rid of the idea that her present trip to the southward was in some way connected with him, and that Pearl Hawlinshed was on board of her.

But he could not disappoint the hungry clubbists again, and he ran the schooner into the bay.

He immediately informed his passengers that he could remain at the port but a few minutes. He was going up to the store to obtain provisions for the boat, and would give them something to eat as soon as she was under way again. Then it appeared that only one of them had any money, — Corny Minkfield, whose mother had given him permission to make the trip over to Plattsburgh, — and he had only half a dollar.

Corny went with Dory to the store. They bought a large supply of bread and crackers, a salt fish, and finally the storekeeper offered to part with a ham he had cooked for the use of his own family. Half a small cheese was added to the stock of provisions, which Dory paid for, and they hastened back to the wharf.

"Have you seen any thing of that steamer?" asked Dory, as he came within hailing distance of his companions.

"She has not shown herself yet," replied Thad.

"We have been gone longer than I intended; for the boiled ham took more time than all the rest of the things," replied Dory, as he and Corny deposited their joint burden on the forward deck of the Goldwing. "The Missisquoi was this side of Crab Island when I saw her, and she can't be far off."

"What do we care for the Missisquoi now?" asked Corny.

"Cast off that bow line, Dick Short," added Dory, without answering the question.

The skipper shoved the schooner off from the wharf, and told Dick to hoist the jib. Heading the Goldwing to the eastward, Dory stood out of the harbor. The boat was hardly under way before the Missisquoi put in an appearance at the northern entrance of the bay. Dory kept on his course after he had calculated the point at which the steamer was likely to come nearest to him.

"There she is!" exclaimed several of the club in the same breath. "She is striking in ahead of us."

The Missisquoi was less than a quarter of a mile from the Goldwing. It could plainly be seen that there were two men in her pilot-house; and Dory was confident that Pearl Hawlinshed was one of them. His intentions were certainly very serious if he had gone to the expense of hiring a steamer to chase him. Probably he had found some way to break up the sale of the Goldwing. But, whatever his mission, the skipper did not want to see him. He was too closely connected with the secret of the night before to come any nearer to him. He decided, that, if the son of his liberal friend succeeded in "interviewing" him, he would have to run for it.

"I don't understand what that fellow wants of you, Dory," said Corny Minkfield.

"And I don't understand it any better than you do," replied Dory. "All I have to say about it is, that I don't like the looks of the fellow, and I mean to keep out of his way. Pass round the grub, Corny."

Dory thought the food would stop their mouths, and it did. His fellow-voyagers asked no more questions, for they were too busy with the provisions to give attention to any thing else.

As the Goldwing went out from the land, she began to feel the force of the wind, and she darted ahead under the influence of the sharp puffs. A few minutes later the Goldwing passed the bow of the Missisquoi not more than forty rods from her.

CHAPTER XI.

THE BEGINNING OF THE CHASE.

"GOLDWING, ahoy!" shouted Pearl Hawlinshed from the bow of the Missisquoi. "I want you, Dory Dornwood!"

The skipper of the Goldwing decided to take no notice of the dangerous man. The other members of the club were so deeply interested in filling their empty stomachs that they gave no attention to the call of Pearl. The provisions had been taken into the cuddy, and Corny was helping his companions. Those who were not in the cabin were sitting on the floor of the standing room, and they could not see the Missisquoi.

"Don't you hear me? I say, I want to see you, Dory Dornwood!" shouted Pearl again with all his might.

Dory could see that those in charge of the Missisquoi were not managing the chase very well. Instead of steering the steamer to a point ahead of the Goldwing, Captain Vesey had run her directly for her. If the schooner had come to when directed to do so, as the captain of her evidently expected, it would have been all right. As it was, the Goldwing had made the eighth of a mile by the blunder.

Dory had practically intimated to his pursuer, that, if he wanted him, he must come after him. He knew that the steamer could not make more than eight miles an hour at her best, and she was not likely to do as well as this in the heavy sea of the lake out from the shore. The skipper of the Goldwing did not expect to outsail the Missisquoi under his present short sail.

When Pearl saw that Dory had no intention of coming to and waiting for him to go on board of the schooner, he called to Captain Vesey to follow the Goldwing. Instead of doing so, he rang his bell to stop the engine. Dory could not hear what passed between the captain and his passenger; but he was aware that an animated discussion was in progress on board of the steamer.

The Goldwing was certainly behaving very well for a boat with such a bad reputation. Dory had been gaining confidence in her ability every moment of the time since she left the breakwater. It was evident to him that sailing on the wind was her weak point, or rather her dangerous one. But she had the wind on her port quarter at present; and Dory did not care to run her directly before the wind, as he would have been obliged to do if he had taken a direct course for Burlington.

The skipper no longer doubted the ability of the Goldwing to cross the lake, violent as the sea was at a distance from the shore. He headed her for Garden Island, nearly half a mile south of Valcour's Island, which sheltered the boat from the full force of the strong wind. From Garden Island to Providence Island, off the south-western extremity of South Hero, it was only two miles and a half. Not more than half of this distance would be through the roughest water; for Valcour's sheltered a considerable portion of the course.

Dory wondered what the discussion between the captain and the passenger of the Missisquoi was all about. He judged that the master of the steamer was not willing to follow the Goldwing any farther. He hoped they would continue the dispute for a while longer. If they did, he should be out of their reach in a short time; for he was confident the schooner was making at least six miles an hour.

But the skipper was not to be fully gratified; for the next time time he looked about at the steamer, she was under way again, and with her bow pointed to the Goldwing. She was half a mile astern of the schooner, and this was a considerable distance for her to gain. But Dory began to feel the excitement of the race, for it was evident that there was to be a race.

The high land at the southern end of Valcour's Island was making it altogether too mild for the Goldwing, for the Missisquoi was evidently gaining very rapidly upon her. Dory started the sheets, and ran to the southward, where he could get more wind. The steamer promptly changed her course, and followed the schooner. It was plain that Captain Vesey or Pearl Hawlinshed, whichever was managing the steamer, had no idea of using any thing like tact or stratagem in the chase. Probably the pilot did not consider that any thing of the kind was necessary, and that the steamer ought to overhaul the sailboat simply by outsailing her.

By this time the other members of the Goldwing Club had eaten all they could, and their occupation became uninteresting. Corny put the provisions into a locker in the cabin, and there was enough left for two or three meals more. First one stood up, and then another, until all had taken a view of the Missisquoi.

"The steamer is chasing you, Dory," said Thad, as though he had made a discovery. "She is following us with all her might."

"I know it," replied Dory, looking behind him at the steamer.

"What is she chasing us for?" asked Corny.

"She wants to catch us," added Dory.

"Is it to find out whether she can beat the Goldwing?" asked Nat. "She's a steamer, and she ought to beat her every time."

"Perhaps she ought to, but I don't intend that she shall."

"You don't expect to run away from a steamer, do you, Dory?" said Dick Short.

"I don't expect to let her catch us; but it will depend upon how fast that steamer can go," added Dory.

"But what does she want to catch us for,

Dory?" persisted Corny, repeating the question he had put before.

"I thought I told you about it. The man in the bow wanted to buy the Goldwing. I bid over him, and got the boat. That made him mad. This is all I know about the reason for his chasing us. He is a wicked fellow, and I think he means to do me harm. All I want to do is to keep out of his way," replied Dory. "I don't know what he wants of me, and you are just as wise as I am. We won't say any thing more about that matter."

"Of course he will catch you," added Thad. "Who ever heard of such a thing as a sailboat running away from a steamer?"

"No matter whether we ever heard of such a thing or not, we are going to try it now," replied Dory. "But I can't have you fellows flying about all over the boat any longer. Two of you sit on each side of me, and I think there will be fun in this thing before we get through with it."

"All right, Dory: you are the captain of this ship, and we will do just what you say," replied Corny.

The boys disposed of themselves as the skipper directed, and sat as still as they could, which was not saying much. But Dory was satisfied that they would keep still enough as soon as the boat got a little more to the eastward, where she would feel the full force of the strong breeze.

"She is gaining on us, Dory," said Thad; and he and his companions were watching the Missisquoi all the time. They were beginning to get excited over the race, though they seemed to be sure that it would soon come to an end by the steamer overtaking the Goldwing.

"I expect her to gain on us while we are here in still water; but I think she will roll a great deal more than the Goldwing when we get out into the lake," replied Dory.

"Creation! didn't she roll coming over from Burlington?" exclaimed Corny. "I thought she was going to roll clear over. Mr. Button the engineer said Captain Vesey did not know how to handle her."

"Don't you expect that the Goldwing will roll in the big waves?" asked Thad.

"Of course she will; but she sits lighter on the water than that steamer, and she won't dive into the waves so deep. But wait, and we shall soon see what we can do," replied Dory. "You fellows have eaten all you can, and I have not had any thing since my breakfast early this morning."

"I will steer for you, Dory, while you eat your dinner," proposed Corny.

"Did you ever steer a sailboat, Corny?" asked Dory with a smile.

"I never did; but I think I can do it," replied the volunteer.

"I would rather have you make a beginning when it don't blow quite so hard. If the Goldwing is going to upset, I want to know how it is done."

No one in the party had ever sailed a boat, and the skipper was not willing to resign the helm to any of them. At his request Corny brought him something to eat, and he disposed of it while he kept his place at the helm. By the time he had finished his first slice of ham, and a corresponding portion of bread and cheese, the Goldwing was up with Garden Island. The skipper, for his own purposes, had run to the west of it. Although he felt like disposing of another slice of ham, he was too much interested in his occupation to attend further to the question of rations just then.

Dory did not tell his companions what he had been thinking about; but he hoped to leave the Missisquoi at this point, or to get a better start of her. He preferred to explain his plan after he had carried it out if it were a success, or to keep silent if it were a failure. He watched the Missisquoi very closely, for his own movements would depend upon hers. There was plenty of water to the northward of the island, but there was a shoal to the southward.

If the captain of the steamer had been wise, if he had had his eyes open, he would have kept to the eastward; but he followed directly in the wake of the Goldwing, and was within less than a quarter of a mile of her.

"Do you know how much water the Missisquoi draws, Thad?" asked Dory, as the Goldwing came up with the island.

"I heard Captain Vesey say that she drew six feet when she had her coal in," replied Thad.

"I heard him say so when we were off Apple-Tree Shoal," added Corny. "I asked him why he didn't go close up to the buoy; and he said there was not more than six feet of water on the shoal, and the boat might touch bottom."

"I thought she didn't draw over five feet. If she draws six, so much the better," added Dory.

"Why is it so much the better, Dory?" asked Thad.

"Hold on all, and don't ask any more questions!" said Dory, laughing. "I have business on my hands just now, and I will tell you all about it in about ten minutes."

The skipper had gybed the boat under the lee of Valcour's; but the wind was too fresh where he was now to repeat the manœuvre. It was a gale in this part of the lake, and the Goldwing worked very lively.

"Corny, I want you to handle that jib-sheet," said he when he was ready for his next move.

"But I don't know how," pleaded Corny.

"Do what I tell you, and do it in a hurry when I give the word. This is the jib-sheet, fast to this cleat. When I shift the helm, the jib will shake. Haul in upon it as fast as you can, and get all you can, and keep it when you get it. I shall do the same with the main-sheet."

The skipper put the helm down.

CHAPTER XII.

A ROUGH TIME OF IT.

THE instant the helm was put down, the head of the boat promptly swung up in the direction of the wind. Both of the sails began to flap and bang in the fierce gale.

"Now haul in, Corny!" said Dory, as he did the same by the main-sheet. "No, Thad! He don't want any help. Let him alone! Take a turn on the cleat," added the skipper, when one of the party wanted to help.

It was necessary only to take in the slack line of the sheet, and no hard pulling was required. The boat was now headed to the westward, which was the opposite course from that which she had been sailing when he headed her to the southward.

"Now we are on the wind, which is said to be the dangerous course in the Goldwing's sailing," added the skipper; and this was the first time he had her close-hauled.

He watched her with the most intense interest, but he had no fault to find with the boat. It took all his strength at the long tiller to keep her from coming up into the wind. There was no lee helm now, with only a jib and mainsail; though she might exhibit this failing when she had all sail on. In fact, she carried too much weather helm; for it impeded her progress.

"She works like a lady!" exclaimed Dory with enthusiasm.

Having satisfied himself in regard to the working of the boat, he turned his attention to the Missisquoi again. He saw that Pearl Hawlinshed was at the wheel of the steamer. He had evidently learned wisdom from the movements of the Goldwing. He had turned the helm of the steamer, so that she was now headed to the westward.

Probably Pearl had begun to do some reasoning by this time. Instead of running directly for the schooner, he had taken a course to intercept her when she attempted to go to the northward, as he doubtless believed she intended to do.

The Goldwing was now on the starboard tack; and the Missisquoi was running abreast of her, towards the west shore of the lake. Dory contrived to cramp her so that she did not make much headway, and the steamer gained so rapidly on her that she was soon a considerable distance ahead of her.

"Now, Dick Short, we are going about. When Corny lets go of the weather jib-sheet, I want you to haul on the lee-sheet," said the skipper when he was ready for the next move.

"Where are we going next, Dory?" asked Thad, confused by the many movements of the skipper.

"No questions now, Thad. Keep your eyes wide open, and you will see for yourself. Let go, and haul! Let go the sheet, Corny! Haul in, Dick! Be lively about it! You must get the sheet in while the sail is shaking, or you can't do it at all," said Dory sharply, as he put the helm down.

The Goldwing whirled around like a top, when her helm went down. The hands in charge of the jib-sheets were zealous to do their duty promptly, and in an instant the sails were drawing on the port tack.

But this did not give the course the skipper

wanted. He handled the boat very cautiously on account of her bad reputation.

Gradually he let off the main-sheet, while Dick was directed to do the same with the jib-sheet. At the same time Dory kept the helm up, and the boat fell off until she was headed for the southern side of Garden Island. She took the wind over her port quarter. It came in heavy gusts, the Goldwing careening until her gunwale went under at every flaw.

"I don't know about this," said Thad.

"About what, Thad?" asked Dory quietly.

"We are about half under water. This is shaky sailing, in my opinion," added Thad, as a wave broke against the side of the boat, and drenched most of the members of the club to the skin.

"We may get wholly under water before we get through with this trip," replied Dory. "But she will come up every time she goes down. For my part, I never saw a boat work any better than the Goldwing is doing."

"But you will drown the whole of us, Dory!" protested Thad.

"She is working first-rate, Thad; and this isn't

more than half as lively as it will be before we get across the lake."

"Are you going across the lake now, Dory?" asked Corny.

"Certainly I am. We are bound for Burlington, aren't we? Didn't you want me to take you home?"

"But we don't want you to drown us, and this boat has a bad habit of not keeping on the top of the water."

"She will keep on the top of the water most of the time, and the worst you have to fear is a wet jacket."

Just as the schooner was going in under the lee of Garden Island, another wave broke against her side, and about half a barrel of water dropped into the standing-room.

"There it is again!" exclaimed Thad.

"That's all right," added Dory. "No boat can keep all the water on the outside of her in such a sea as this. But she is working beautifully. Do you see that rope, Thad?" continued the skipper, pointing to the line by which the centre-board was handled.

"I see it, but I haven't the least idea what it is for."

"I want you and Nat to haul up the centre-board, for we don't need quite so much of it while we are going free."

The two boys named cast off the line, and pulled with all their might; but they could not start the board, as Dory did not suppose they could while the whole force of the wind was acting against it. The two hands at the line did not know what the centre-board was, or where it was; but the skipper thought, as they seemed to be a little concerned about their safety, that it was better for them to be employed.

"It's no use!" cried Thad. "I don't know what we are pulling at; but, whatever it is, it won't come."

"What is there down there?" asked Nat Long, looking into the pump, which was at the end of the centre-board casing.

"Now try it once more, fellows," said Dory, as he luffed the boat up, and thus relieved the centre-board from the pressure.

"Now it comes," added Thad. "Shall we haul the thing through that hole?"

"No: that will do. Make the line fast to the cleat, as you found it."

"But what does all that mean? I never saw a boat that had a thing like that in it," inquired Nat Long.

"You will learn all about it by and by. I have no time now to explain any thing," answered Dory, looking behind him to ascertain the position of the Missisquoi.

The steamer had come about. Pearl had found that he had been reckoning wrong in regard to the movements of the Goldwing. Judging from his present career, he was disgusted with strategy; for he was again running directly for the schooner. The Missisquoi was laboring heavily in the big waves, and her pilot did not appear to know how to favor her. At any rate, he followed the schooner without regard to the wind or the waves.

"She is after us," said Corny, as the Goldwing went into the comparatively smooth water under the lee of Garden Island. "She is going to catch us, too, in the course of the next fifteen minutes."

"When she catches us, you tell me of it: will you, Corny?" added Dory.

"I think you will know it as well as I do, Dory. What's the use of keeping this thing up?

Let us hold on, and see what the fellow wants of you," replied Corny.

"We will have the fun of the race if we don't have any thing more," said Dory. "This is smooth sailing just here, but we shall have it rough enough in about two minutes more. If any of you fellows don't want to go back to Burlington, I will put you on shore at Garden Island."

"We might have to stay there a week," suggested Corny.

"I couldn't help that," answered Dory. "I told you not to come with me if you were afraid of the boat."

"She is as safe for us as she is for Dory," added Dick Short.

"We shall get under the lee of Providence Island in about twenty minutes. If you can stand it for that time, you will be all right," continued the skipper, who did not wish to waste his time, and lose the race, by putting any of his crew on shore.

"I don't want to go ashore," said Nat Long. "I can stand it as long as Dory can, and I shall not back out."

This exhibition of pluck had its effect on the

others, and no one was willing to admit that he wished to go ashore. But the appearance of the lake ahead was appalling to most of them, though they had crossed it that day in the little steamer. The bad reputation of the Goldwing was what made it look so dubious. Dory had been as doubtful about crossing as any of them; but he had tested the boat under her present sail, and all his doubts had been removed. For a boy of his age he had had a great deal of experience in sailing a boat; and he knew by the feeling, rather than by any thing he could see, that the schooner was working well. He believed that she was entirely safe.

He had ascertained the draught of the Goldwing at the wharf, and he was perfectly familiar with every part of the lake. When the boat came up with the island, he ran within a few rods of it. He looked astern at the Missisquoi as he came into the still water under the lee of the island. She had been gaining rapidly upon him; and, if his strategy failed, Pearl Hawlinshed would soon be alongside of the Goldwing.

But he could hardly conceive of such a thing as its failing. He watched the steamer with the most intense interest as he increased his distance from the island. The schooner passed out into the open lake. The gusts of wind increased in fury, and even the reefed mainsail seemed to be more sail than she could carry.

More than once, under the pressure of the savage gusts, the boat heeled down till the water rolled in over the lee gunwale. The heavy waves broke continually over the other side; and, before the Goldwing was half way across the open part of the lake, the water rose above her bottom boards.

"This is awful, Dory," said Thad. "I don't believe we shall ever get to the other side of the lake. If I had thought it was half as bad as this, I wouldn't have come."

"It is very wet; and that is the worst you can say of it," replied Dory. "We are going over all right, but we must keep more of this water on the outside of the boat. Thad, you may man the pump; for it is getting rather damp in the standing-room."

The members of the Goldwing Club looked decidedly shaky, with the exception of the skipper. No one responded to the timid sentiment of

Thad; but probably all of them felt it, and wished they were on shore, though that shore were the one they had just left.

"The Missisquoi has stopped!" cried Corny, when the Goldwing was about half way over to Providence Island. "She has chosen a quiet place under the lee of that little island."

"She has stopped, that's a fact," added Thad.

"I thought she would," replied Dory, as he let off the sheet when a heavy gust struck the sails. "The Missisquoi is aground."

CHAPTER XIII.

SAFE UNDER A LEE.

"HOW do you know she is aground, Dory?" asked Corny, after a careful examination of the position of the Missisquoi.

"She wouldn't have stopped there if she hadn't got aground. She has done the very thing I wanted her to do, and the very thing I did my best to have her do," replied Dory triumphantly.

"Do you mean to say that you did it, Dory?" asked Thad, still pumping away with all his might.

"I don't mean to say that I got the steamer aground. I saw that neither Captain Vesey nor the other fellow knew much about the lake; for the Missisquoi followed the Goldwing wherever she went," Dory explained. "I ran close to the island, hoping the steamer would follow me, as she has been doing, because there is not more than four feet of water close up to the land where I went. She had either to follow us in a straight line, or to go to the southward of the shoal. I was sure to make something in getting away from her."

"What will she do now?" inquired Dick Short.

"She must either work off the shoal, or stay there; and I am sure I don't care what she does," added Dory, as he looked ahead at the savage waves that were piling up in the path of the schooner.

The Goldwing was more than half way across the lake: and, the farther she went, the rougher the lake was; for the longer was the sweep of the wind. But Dory was not in a hurry when he found the steamer could no longer follow him. He had been very careful not to lose any thing by letting off the main-sheet, except when it was absolutely necessary to do so in order to keep the boat right side up.

Going nearly before the wind, it took a long sweep to reduce the pressure on the mainsail; and the water flowed in over the lee side about as fast as Thad could pump it out. The boys looked at each other, and there is no doubt that they all wished they were on shore. They kept an eye on the skipper's face, to note any anxiety or alarm on his part. Dory was confident the boat would not take in water enough to swamp her while he could control her with the helm; but he felt that he had his hands full, and that he should be very fortunate if nothing happened to cripple the boat.

"I have got about enough of this thing," said Thad.

"Nat, you take Thad's place at the pump," interposed Dory. "One hand needn't do all the hard work."

"All right! I am ready to do my share of the work," replied Nat, as he took Thad's place at the pump.

"I didn't mean that. I am not tired," added Thad. "The farther we go the worse it is, Dory; and I have had about enough of this sort of sailing."

"Well, what are you going to do about it?" asked Dory pleasantly. "Are you going to get out, and walk the rest of the way? Or will you swim ashore? I don't think you will find it is any easier walking or swimming, or any safer."

"Can't we turn about and go back?" inquired

Thad, looking with dismay at the waves ahead, and at the water that poured in over both rails.

"We are more than half way over, and it is hardly worth while to go about," replied Dory. "If we return, we shall have to beat back; but we are in no hurry now, and perhaps we can ease off a little more."

"I don't see how you are going to ease off, Dory," said Thad. "Here we are right in the thick of it; and we must take it as it comes, unless you go back."

"Do you see those cleats on the mainmast, Thad?" asked Dory, making ready to do something,—"one on each side of the mast, with a rope leading up? Do you see them?"

"I don't know what cleats are," answered Thad.

"Those brass things, with ropes around them."

"I see them. These are what you hoist the sail with," added Thad, as he grasped the ropes.

"Now let go both ropes together when I give the word. Not yet! All the rest of you, grab the sail when it comes down, and mind the gaff don't hit you in the head."

"What are you going to do, Dory?" asked Thad. "I have the ropes in my hands."

"I am going to take in the mainsail. That will ease her off; and I can work her before it with the jib alone."

At this moment a tremendous gust struck the mainsail, and Dory crowded the helm down; but the schooner took in a large quantity of water over the lee side as she careened.

"Let go the halyards, Thad!" shouted the skipper as the boat swept around. "Look out for the sail, all of you!"

But the sail did not readily come down, the pressure upon it causing it to bind. But Dory continued to luff until it was released.

"Haul down the sail lively!" called Dory with energy, when the canvas began to thrash and beat about as though it was bound to tear itself into shreds.

Under the direction of the skipper the sail was secured after a great deal of difficulty. Dory let her off again under the jib alone. This proved to be a decided change for the better. The Gold-wing kept on a tolerably even keel, and drove ahead almost as fast as she did before.

"She's doing a good deal better," said Thad, who began to breathe freer than he had since the boat went into the worst of it. "Why didn't we do that before?"

"Because we were trying to keep out of the way of the Missisquoi before," replied Dory.

But it was not baby play, even with nothing but the jib set. The mainsail had steadied the boat to some extent; but now she began to roll tremendously, and was not so readily controlled by the helm. The waves broke over her on the weather side, but she did not scoop up the water on the lee side.

The Goldwing had taken in so much water that it was swashing about in the standing-room. Dory directed Nat to keep pumping. Dick Short was told to take a pail which belonged to the boat, and Corny was armed with a tin dipper. The members of the club were glad to have something to do, as almost any nervous person is; and they worked with tremendous zeal. In a short time the pump sucked, and not another dipperful of water could be taken up in the well.

"Now we are all right," said Dory. "We can take it easy now."

"We are almost over to Providence Island," added Corny.

"We shall be in smooth water in ten minutes more."

"But we are a long way from Burlington," suggested Thad.

"At least a dozen miles," said the skipper. "Of course you know that we can't get there, fellows, without going outside of Colchester Point. All the rest of the way is quite as bad as, if not worse than, we have been having for the last twenty minutes."

"Are we going right along to Burlington, Dory?" asked Thad in dismay at the information given by the skipper.

"I think not at present," replied Dory. "But you have been through this once before to-day."

"It wasn't half so bad as it is now," protested Corny. "It didn't begin to blow very hard until we got to Valcour's Island."

"Did the Missisquoi make better weather of it than the Goldwing?" asked Dory.

"The lake didn't begin to be as rough as it was a little while ago," replied Corny. "The steamer pitched tremendously, and we all had to pump after we got beyond Valcour's."

"Do you see any thing of the Missisquoi?"

asked Dory, who had been too busy to give any attention to the steamer.

"I can just see her at the south of the island. She has not got off yet," replied Corny.

"She is under the lee of the two islands; and they can be very comfortable on board of her for the rest of the day, — a great deal more comfortable than they would be out in the lake where we have been," added Dory.

The Goldwing was abreast of Providence Island by this time. The waves swept furiously along the south-west shore of the land.

As soon as she reached the south-east point, the skipper luffed up; but the boat was not inclined to make any headway on the new course.

"Let off the centre-board, Thad," said the skipper, as the boat began to make more leeway than headway.

Thad had got the hang of this rope; and, as the centre-board went down, the boat came up to the work. With the help of an oar and a great deal of coaxing, the skipper got her close up to the shore in seven feet of water. He had instructed Corny how to get the anchor overboard. The boat was entirely out of the heavy sea, though the water rose and fell under the influence of the waves which were rolling along the other side of the island.

"Here we are as safe as though we had the boat on the top of Mansfield Mountain," said Dory, after he had secured the cable, and stowed the jib.

"I never expected to come out of it alive," said Thad, as the skipper seated himself in the standing-room to recover from the excitement of the perilous run across the lake.

"Nor I either," added Nat Long.

"It looked very shaky," said Corny; "but I didn't give it up at any time."

"Now, really, Dory, did you expect to get out of that scrape?" asked Thad. "Be honest about it, and tell us what you actually thought."

"Of course I knew that something might break, just as I know that a horse may run away with me when I'm out riding. The wagon or the harness might break, and that would spoil the best calculation," replied Dory.

"But, without any thing breaking, didn't you expect the boat would go to the bottom?" urged Thad.

"I didn't expect any thing of the kind. I have been out in a sailboat when it was as bad or worse than it is to-day. If nothing broke, I knew we should come out of it all right; and I never thought of such a thing as going to the bottom. It looks a good deal worse to you fellows who were never out in a sailboat when it blew hard than it really is. I didn't think there was any great danger when we started out: if I had, I shouldn't have come over," said Dory quietly.

The members of the Goldwing Club had the idea that they had had a narrow escape, and the skipper was not inclined to allow them to make heroes of themselves. The motion of a boat in a heavy sea seems terrible to those who are not accustomed to it, and the boys were disposed to make the worst of it.

"I wouldn't try it again if you would give me the Goldwing," said Thad with emphasis.

"After you have been through that sort of thing a few times, you will not mind it at all. It was what I call a lively time: that's all," added Dory. "I went down to St. John with Bill Pitts in a sailboat, and we had a rougher time than this all one day."

Dory thought he should like the rest of his dinner by this time.

CHAPTER XIV.

EARLY IN THE MORNING.

THE skipper of the Goldwing had an excellent appetite, and the other members of the club had regained theirs by this time.

Fortunately they had plenty of provisions, for there was nothing for them to do but eat during the rest of the day. It continued to blow as fresh as it had since the middle of the forenoon till dark.

Dory thought it would abate at night, but there were no signs of a change. The party were pretty thoroughly tired out after the labor and the excitement of the day. The boys gaped until they had nearly thrown their jaws out of joint.

There was room enough in the cabin for four of the club, — two in the berths, and two on the floor between them. Dory decided to sleep in the standing-room, where he was most likely to be waked by any change in the position of the schooner. By eight o'clock all hands were fast asleep. Half of them had nothing better than "the soft side of a board" to sleep on, but they were too tired to need beds of down.

The skipper was the most wakeful sleeper in the party, but he slept for several hours without waking. When he did wake, he sprang to his feet as if conscious that he had neglected his duty as a faithful skipper. He had no idea of what time it was when he sprang to his feet. All was still around him, and the Goldwing appeared to be in precisely the position he had left her when he turned in.

He could no longer hear the roar of the big waves as they dashed against the south side of the island. The violent wind had subsided, and the lake seemed to be as calm as the dream of an infant.

He looked all about him in the darkness, but there was nothing to demand his attention. His companions were all sleeping, and some of them were snoring, on their hard beds. Dory began to gape when there proved to be no grounds for excitement. He concluded that he could not do any better than finish his night's rest. Taking the most comfortable position he could find in the standing-room, he turned in again, and was soon fast asleep.

When he woke in the morning, it was after sunrise. The rest of the club were still fast asleep. The skipper felt like a new man after his long rest. A gentle breeze was rippling the surface of the lake. It came from the westward, and the promise was that the day would be fine. Without calling his companions, he loosed the sails, and turned out the reefs from the fore and main sails. He laced on the bonnet of the jib, and shipped the short tiller, instead of the long one he had used the day before.

So far he had not seen how the sails set when all spread, and he was interested in his present operation. He hoisted the mainsail. It was not so large but that he could handle the throat and peak halyards at the same time. He was entirely satisfied with the set of this sail. The set of the foresail pleased him equally well.

The anchor-rope was rove through a block made fast near the heel of the bowsprit, so that the anchor could be weighed without any difficulty. He succeeded in getting it up without waking his shipmates, though he took no especial pains to avoid arousing them. They had got up at four o'clock the morning before, and probably had not slept much lest they should oversleep themselves, and lose the excursion to Plattsburgh.

Dory hoisted the jib. He was delighted with the appearance of the Goldwing with all sail set. There was hardly a puff of air behind the island, and it was some time before he got fairly under way. But he enjoyed the sight of the boat so much, that he was in no haste to get home. So far as he knew, his mother supposed that he was still waiting on the table in the cabin of the steamer; and she could not be anxious about him. He had not heard of the loss of the Au Sable, and he had no suspicion that his father was not still piloting her up and down the lake.

After a while he succeeded in getting to the southward of Providence Island, so that he could catch the breeze from across the lake. He got just enough to fill the sails; and this afforded him the opportunity to test the working of the boat after he had shifted the ballast, and changed the position of the foremast. There was hardly wind enough for a fair test, but he was delighted to find that the boat carried a weather helm.

As he went farther out from the land, he got more breeze; and the result was entirely satisfactory. Indeed, he had been practically sure that he could remedy the defect in the working of the Goldwing before he bought her. If he failed to do so, he had thrown his money away; for parties would not employ him if he had an unsafe boat. He intended to invite two or three prominent boatmen to sail with him when he had put the boat in first-rate condition, and get their opinion as to her safety and her sailing qualities.

Dory was so much absorbed in the beautiful appearance of the Goldwing, that he neglected to do what an old sailor is continually doing when afloat. He had not looked about him to see what beside the Goldwing was afloat on the lake. He had headed the boat to the south, so as to pass to the west of Stave Island. He was looking ahead, and dreaming of the future.

In the quiet of the still morning he heard a puffing sound at a distance. He turned to see what it was, and discovered a small steamer about a mile to the westward of him. He had seen a boat in that direction when he came out from behind the island, but he took no notice of her. He had forgotten all about the Missisquoi: he had not even thought to look and see if she was still aground on the Garden Island shoal.

The sight of the little steamer, like a dozen others on the lake, reminded him of his pursuer of the day before. He looked with interest in the direction of Garden Island. The Missisquoi was not there. She had got out of that scrape. Then he noticed that the little steamer in the middle of the lake was headed directly for the Goldwing. She looked just like his late pursuer.

Dory was rather excited at the thought of a continuance of the chase; for with the light breeze he had no chance at all, and he did not like to come in collision with Pearl Hawlinshed. He looked the boat over very carefully. He had often sailed in her, and steered her; but she was too far off for him to be entirely sure in regard to her identity. But he was confident that it was the Missisquoi.

Certainly Pearl Hawlinshed had some very strong motive for continuing the chase a second day. What could he want of him? Dory concluded that he either expected to recover the Goldwing, or that he connected him in some manner with his father. Whatever his motive, Dory did not want to see him.

He was confident that the steamer he saw was the Missisquoi, and that Pearl was still in pursuit of him. He had led the steamer into a trap the day before, and possibly he might do it again. He could at least run into shoal-water, where the Missisquoi could not follow him. He was familiar with the soundings in all parts of the lake, for his father had instructed him in the navigation.

Dory was assured that the wind would freshen as the sun rose higher; but it would make little difference to him how much wind there was by and by, if the steamer overhauled him before it came. He thought he was making about four miles an hour, but the steamer was good for at least six. She had a mile to gain, and that would take her ten minutes. Following out the calculation, Dory thought the steamer would overhaul him in fifteen minutes. In that time he could make a mile.

"Hallo, Dory! You are up and dressed," exclaimed Thad Glovering, thrusting his head out at the cabin-door.

"Dry up, Thad! I am busy now," replied Dory impatiently; for he was in the midst of his calculation of what he should do to avoid the Missisquoi.

"You don't seem to be doing any thing, Dory," added Thad, as his body followed his head out at the door.

"Don't disturb me, please, but call the fellows. I want them in the standing-room, so as to trim the boat, and make her sail better," answered the skipper, as he went on with his calculation.

He had time to make only a mile before the steamer would be down upon him. He was about abreast of Stave Island now. Less than a mile south of it were two ledges, on which the water was not more than six feet deep. Going to the southward, vessels must keep Juniper Light open to the westward of Colchester Reef Light, in order to avoid these reefs. There were no buoys on them, for they lay outside of any usual course of vessels bound up and down the lake.

The experience of the Missisquoi in getting aground the day before would render her pilot wary about following the Goldwing. The two reefs were half a mile apart; and the pursuer must either keep away from them, or run the risk of getting aground on one of them. The Goldwing could go over either of them in perfect safety, for she drew only three feet with her board up.

Dory was satisfied with his calculation, and he was reasonably confident that the Missisquoi would not get within a quarter of a mile of the Goldwing; but, if this expedient failed, he had another to which he intended to resort.

The other members of the club had come out into the standing-room, and seated themselves as they had been required to do the day before. They were all wide awake; but they had been cautioned by Thad not to disturb the skipper, and they were silent till he spoke to them.

"You have come to life again, fellows," said he when he had fully arranged his plan.

"So have you, Dory," replied Corny. "Thad said we were not to speak to you, or we should bust your calculations. We all thought you had the blues."

"I suppose you know the steamer that is following the Goldwing," replied Dory. "It is the

Missisquoi, and she is after us again to-day. I have been thinking how we should keep out of her way."

"How are you going to do it?" asked Corny. "We may enjoy the fun if we know something about it."

The skipper explained his plan in full, and his companions were quite interested in it. There was no chance for a race while only a four-knot breeze favored the Goldwing. With a good stiff breeze the skipper believed he could beat the steamer; but, in the absence of such a wind, he must resort to strategy. But strategy was quite as exciting to his companions as a race. It afforded the opportunity for one craft to come out better than the other.

The wind was sensibly freshening, but the Goldwing did not need any more wind just then. She was almost up with Stave Island Ledge, and her skipper was disposed to wait and see what his pursuer would do. As he approached the dangerous reef, — dangerous to any craft drawing more than five feet, — he started his sheets, and stood to the eastward of the rocks.

The Missisquoi was within an eighth of a mile

of the Goldwing, and the skipper saw that Captain Vesey was at the wheel. He seemed to know about the reef, and sheered off. Probably he had discovered by this time that Pearl Hawlinshed knew even less than he did about the difficulties of navigation in Lake Champlain.

CHAPTER XV.

THE STRATEGY OF THE CHASE.

DORY DORNWOOD had accomplished all that he intended by his plan. The pilot of the Missisquoi would not dare to cross the ledges, and it would be necessary for her to go nearly a mile to the southward to get around them. Dory calculated that his manœuvre had given him two miles the start of the steamer.

Captain Vesey and Pearl Hawlinshed seemed to be holding a consultation. Dory imagined that Pearl was trying to persuade the captain to venture in among the rocks. If so, he was not successful; for the Missisquoi did not come any nearer to the ledge.

"What is she going to do next, Dory?" asked Corny Minkfield, while the boys were waiting for the next move of the steamer.

"That's more than I know," replied Dory, chuckling at the success of his plan. "I think

Captain Vesey had enough of getting aground yesterday, and he don't want to spend the day laid up on one of these ledges. I believe the steamer would go over Champion Rock all right; but her captain is shy, and I don't think he will come any nearer than he is now."

Dory had headed the Goldwing to the east. As he had predicted, the wind was increasing, and the schooner carried quite a bone in her teeth. It looked a little like a game of chess, where each player has to wait a long time for the other to make his move. The captain and his passenger appeared to be still engaged in the discussion in the bow of the boat. Dory thought he could quicken their movements; and, hauling in his sheets, he stood to the south.

"There she goes!" exclaimed Thad, as the steamer started her propeller again.

"I think we can keep her moving," replied Dory. "She will go to the southward as fast as we do, to head us off. We can play this game as long as she can."

"But who wants to stay here all day fooling with that steamer?" said Corny.

"I don't know that we have any thing better

to do," added Dick Short. "We have got enough to eat to last us all day."

"I think we shall have some variety in this thing. Captain Vesey has to deliver the Missisquoi to her new owner to-night, and he can't stay here much after noon," replied Dory.

In fifteen minutes the steamer was well to the southward of Champion Rock, and began to turn to the eastward.

"She is coming around to pick us up on this side of the rocks," said Thad.

"That's all right, but she won't pick us up," answered Dory. "I am afraid it will get very monotonous before she overhauls us by her present tactics."

Dory put the boat about, and stood to the north. He continued on this tack until the Missisquoi was directly south of Stave Island, and of both ledges, which were in a line with the island. She had gone half a mile farther to the southward than was necessary to avoid Champion Rock; but her pilots were not well posted, and they seemed to be determined to keep on the safe side.

The skipper waited until the steamer was half

a mile to the eastward of the ledges, and then he proceeded to beat across the dangerous ground. He took a southerly tack first, so as to bother the pilot of the steamer as to his intentions. The Missisquoi kept on her course, and Pearl was evidently bothered.

The pursuer had not thought there could be any difficulty in capturing the owner of the Goldwing when he had a steamer to use in chasing her. He had found out his mistake. The captain and engineer had not earned their five dollars apiece yet, for they had not put the passenger on board of the schooner. Doubtless they were continuing the chase for the purpose of obtaining their money, for the boys were satisfied that Captain Vesey had no other interest in the pursuit.

As the Missisquoi put her helm to starboard, in order to run to the north, Dory tacked the schooner, and stood off to the north-east. This course would carry him directly over Stave Island Ledge. The effect of this move was soon apparent, for the steamer stopped her screw again. Her pilots could see that it was useless to go any farther on her present course. By the time she got a mile farther, the Goldwing would be on the other side of the ledges. Another discussion seemed to be in progress between the captain and the passenger. But it was not continued long; for the Missisquoi put about, and stood to the westward.

"She has got enough of that," said Thad. "I don't believe she will keep it up much longer."

"It is cool and comfortable here, and I think we can stand this sort of thing as long as she can," added Dory.

"Of course we can; but the game is ended, and the Missisquoi is going back to Plattsburgh," suggested Corny.

"The game is not ended yet," replied Dory: "in fact, it has but just begun."

"What's the reason it isn't ended?" demanded Corny, who did not like to have his conclusions disputed. "What is the steamer going off in that direction for, if there is to be any more fun?"

"Is that the way to Plattsburgh, Corny?" asked Dory quietly.

"She has gone off and left us, whether she is bound to Plattsburgh or not. If she means to catch us, why don't she stick to it?" continued Corny.

"She is sticking to it. The way to catch a pigeon is to put salt on his tail, you know," answered Dory, laughing. "She is beginning to play her game now. If she had gone to the north-west, instead of to the west, I might believe she had given it up; and I should be ready to head the Goldwing for Burlington as soon as I saw her to the eastward of Valcour's Island."

"What do you think she means to do, Dory?" asked Thad.

"I am very clear what she means to do. I wouldn't give anybody two cents to write it down for me," replied the skipper confidently. "She has gone to the west so that she can coax us out from these ledges. If she could get us away from these dangers, where she could chase us, she would soon be up with us."

"There are plenty of rocks and shoals south of us," suggested Thad.

"But there are buoys on them, and a hundred feet of water between them. Very likely Captain Vesey knows his way among them. We can very soon see whether she has given up the chase or not," said Dory, as he put the boat about, and headed her to the south.

"Are you going to run for Burlington, Dory?" asked Corny.

"We are headed in that direction now," replied the skipper.

"But the steamer does not change her course," continued Corny.

"And she won't change her course until we have gone a couple of miles farther to the southward. They are getting smart on board of the Missisquoi," added Dory, like one who is driving a winning horse.

All hands watched the steamer very closely, and Corny would have given something handsome to have it made out that Dory was mistaken in his calculations. He was loyal to the skipper, but he did not like to have statements of the latter prove true every time. The steamer did not change her course, but she did not seem to get ahead very fast.

In half an hour the Goldwing was off Colchester Reef Light. The Missisquoi was still headed to the west; and Corny was beginning to feel triumphant, though he was not confident enough to say much. The steamer was three miles distant; but Dory was satisfied by this time that she had stopped her propeller, and was only waiting for the schooner to get a little farther to the southward, where she could not dodge in among the dangerous rocks.

"She is coming about!" shouted Thad.

"It is about time for her to do something," replied Dory. "But she is not coming down this way."

"How do you know she isn't, Dory Dornwood?" demanded Corny, who was rather indignant when the skipper made another prediction.

"I think I understand her little game," answered Dory mildly; for he felt that he could afford to disregard the sharp tones of Corny.

"Where is she going?" asked Corny, wishing to make the skipper commit himself fully.

"She is going to the eastward," replied Dory without any hesitation; for it was all a plain case to him.

"How do you know she is, Dory?" demanded Corny. "She is still turning; and she isn't headed any way yet."

"I think it is easy enough to see what she is

about, Corny. Can't you see it with your eyes shut?"

"No: I'm sure I can't; and I don't believe you can, Dory Dornwood," added Corny.

"She is now just as far west of Champion Rock as we are south of it. She is going to the eastward, so as to cut us off if we try to reach the ledges again. I think she has got her course now."

It was plain enough to all the members of the Goldwing Club, that, as they could see the whole of the starboard side of the Missisquoi, she was headed to the eastward. Corny gave it up when he saw that he could hold out no longer. From the smoke that poured out of the smoke-stack of the little steamer, it was plain that she was crowded to her best speed.

"She is in a hurry now," said the skipper, laughing.

"She is going to do a big thing now," added Thad. "She is going to catch us, sure."

"But I think we had better be doing something," continued the skipper, as he put the Goldwing before the wind.

"What are you going to do now, Dory?" asked Corny.

"That will depend upon circumstances," replied Dory, who suddenly appeared to be disposed to keep his own counsel.

As soon as the schooner was up with the light-house, the skipper hauled in his sheets again, and headed the Goldwing to the north-east. This course seemed to bother the steamer, for it made it evident that the boat did not intend to go near Champion Rock.

"She's after you again," said Corny a few minutes later. "She has altered her course, and is coming down this way to head you off."

"All right! Let her come," replied Dory.

"But we are getting pretty close together," added Thad. "She is going to catch us this time. At least, I am afraid she is."

"Don't worry about it, Thad. She isn't going to catch us on this tack."

The Missisquoi was coming in between Hog's Back Island and the reef of the same name. She kept the red buoy on her starboard, and the black on her port hand. She was hardly more than a quarter of a mile from the Goldwing, and running for a point ahead of her. It began to be very exciting for the boys, for they believed she would overtake the schooner in a few minutes more.

But the Goldwing came out just a little ahead; and the steamer was astern of the boat, but not more than a hundred yards. She gained on her every minute, until suddenly the Missisquoi stopped.

CHAPTER XVI.

A GRAVE CHARGE AGAINST THE SKIPPER.

THE Missisquoi was aground. This result was exactly what the skipper of the Goldwing intended and expected, if the pilots of the steamer followed the schooner. Colchester Light is about west of a point having the same name. Extending north from Colchester Point is a shoal, on which, at the present low stage of the water, there was a depth of from two to eight feet. It was two miles and a half long from its northern extremity to the point.

Dory struck the shoal not more than a quarter of a mile north of Law Island, where the water was only about four feet deep. The Goldwing went over it without any difficulty; but there was not water enough for the steamer. Ordinarily a small steamer could have crossed any part of the shoal, but the lake had not been so low before for years.

The skipper of the schooner had calculated upon using this shoal in the same manner that he had used Champion Rock and Stave Island Ledge. If he had not depended upon this shallow water, he would not have left the ledges. But he did not expect that Captain Vesey would attempt to follow him where there was not more than four feet of water. It was evident enough that neither the captain nor Pearl was a competent pilot.

"Here we are," said Dory quietly, as he put the helm down, and came up into the wind.

"What's the matter now?" asked Corny.

"Nothing the matter; but the Missisquoi has concluded not to come any farther in this direction just now," replied Dory, as he headed the schooner to the north-west.

"She has stopped!" exclaimed Thad.

"That is just what she has done," added the skipper.

"What has she stopped there for?" asked Corny.

"She couldn't very well help it, for she is hugging the bottom."

"Hugging the bottom! What do you mean by that?" demanded Corny.

"In plain English, she is aground." And the skipper proceeded to explain the situation to his companions.

"Then, you knew what you were about all the time, Dory," said Thad, with something of admiration in his tones and manner.

"I thought I did all the time; but I did not expect the Missisquoi would try to go over a place where the bottom is so near the top as it is on this shoal," answered Dory. "There is nearly seven miles of deep water to the eastward of this shoal to the head of Mallett's Bay. The lake is thirteen miles wide on just this line."

"Were you going up Mallett's Bay?"

"Not at all. I expected to run back and forth over this shoal until the Missisquoi had enough of it, and then I was going to Burlington."

"Will the steamer get off the bottom?"

"She was running at her best speed when she struck the bottom; and I don't believe she will get off in a hurry," replied Dory.

"All we have to do is to go to Burlington, then," added Corny.

"We won't be in a hurry about it," said Dory. "I want to see if she can get off. They are backing her now, and there is Captain Vesey at work with a pole. The steamer seems to stick hard. Her bow is about a foot out of water, but I think she is afloat at the stern. They may work her off if they manage it well."

"That other chap has gone to work with a pole too," said Dick Short.

"I hope they will have a good time," added Dory, as he put the schooner about, and headed her across the bow of the Missisquoi.

The skipper wished to obtain a better view of the position of the steamer, to enable him to decide whether it was safe for him to proceed to Burlington. With the wind on the quarter, he ran within ten yards of the stem of the Missisquoi. As he approached her, he saw that her water-line was lifted at least a foot above the surface of the lake, indicating that she was firmly fixed on the hard bottom.

"Hallo there, Dory Dornwood!" shouted Pearl Hawlinshed when the Goldwing came within hail of the steamer. "Come alongside! I want to see you."

"What do you want of me?" asked the skipper.

"I want to see you about that money," added Pearl.

"What money?"

"You know what money as well as I do!" roared Pearl with a string of oaths. "The money you stole at the hotel!"

"The money Dory stole!" ejaculated Corny Minkfield, with a look of horror on his face.

"What hotel? I didn't steal any money at any hotel," returned Dory, startled at the charge.

"Yes, you did! It's no use to deny it. The landlord sent me off after you; and you'll have to pay for it, for the wild-goose chase you have led me on," cried Pearl, who had evidently lost his patience and his temper.

"I didn't know any money had been stolen from a hotel; and I didn't steal it," cried Dory, as the Goldwing passed out of easy talking distance from the steamer.

"You stole the money to buy that boat, and it's no sale!" yelled Pearl.

"Stole the money to buy the boat!" exclaimed Corny, looking at his fellow-members of the Goldwing Club.

"I don't believe it!" ejaculated Thad Glovering. "Dory isn't that kind of a fellow. He wouldn't do such a thing."

Nat Long and Dick Short said nothing. They seemed to be in doubt. All of them wondered where Dory could have got the money to pay for the Goldwing, and the charge of Pearl Hawlinshed appeared to explain the whole matter. Certainly the astonishing statement of Pearl made it look very bad for the skipper of the Goldwing. When they asked where he got the forty-two dollars to pay for the boat, Dory had refused to explain, and had insisted that no more questions should be asked about the subject.

Nat had winked at Corny to intimate that this disposition of the matter was not satisfactory; but, as they were expecting a fine sail in the schooner, they had been politic enough to keep silence. Now they looked from one to another, for they did not like to say just what they thought.

Dory was silent also. His heart was swelling with emotion. He was accused of stealing, and he could not help seeing that he was in a very uncomfortable situation. Pearl's father had given him the money, and he had promised not to say a word about it. There seemed to be some terrible secret between Pearl and his father. The latter had given Dory one hundred and five dollars for the service he had rendered him in the woods, and wished him not to tell where he got the money lest it should lead to the exposure of the secret.

Pearl evidently had something against him. It might be nothing more than the fact that he had outbid him at the sale of the boat. But the son plainly suspected that Dory had some relations with his father, for he had intimated as much as this.

The skipper of the Goldwing was considering what he should do. He was ready to meet the charge against him, though he could not explain where he got the money to pay for the boat. Pearl was after him for stealing the money at a hotel, — what hotel he did not know. Was Pearl a constable or a police-officer?

If his pursuer was an officer of the law, he was ready to give himself up. He was anxious to know in what manner he was connected with the theft. But it might be all a trick on the part of Pearl to get the boat away from him. He did not mean to put his head into any trap. While he was considering the situation, Corny could hold in no longer.

"I want to know about this business," said Corny, after he and his companions had been looking at each other in silence for full five minutes.

"What do you want to know, Corny?" asked Dory.

"I want to know where you got the money to buy this boat," replied Corny, rather more warmly than the occasion seemed to require.

"I shall not tell you," answered Dory firmly, but very quietly.

"You won't?"

"No, I won't," repeated Dory. "That is my secret. I have to keep it, not on my own account, but for the sake of a person who was very kind to me, and gave me a meal when I was hungry. That is all I can say about the case. I didn't steal a dollar or a cent, and I am willing to face any man that says I did."

"That fellow in the steamer says you did; and we have been running away from him since yesterday morning," replied Corny.

"That man, whose name is Pearl Hawlinshed,

has something against me; and I don't care about putting myself into his hands," answered Dory.

"I suppose you don't," added Corny with a sneer. "I don't like this thing a bit. We have been with you since yesterday morning, and they say the receiver is as bad as the thief."

"Do you believe I am a thief, Corny?" said Dory, looking his accuser squarely in the eye.

"I don't see how I can believe any thing else. I don't want to believe such a thing of you, Dory. Fellows like you and me don't have forty-two dollars in every pocket of their trousers; and you won't tell us where you got the money," answered Corny a little more moderately.

"You talk and act just as though you did want to prove that I stole the money I paid for the boat," added Dory. "All I ask of the fellows is to believe that I am innocent until I am proved guilty."

"That's the talk! that's fair! I don't believe Dory did it!" exclaimed Thad.

"Let him tell where he got the money, then," replied Corny.

"That's his business, if he don't choose to tell,"

argued Thad. "It don't prove that Dory is a thief because that fellow says so. We don't know any thing about that fellow."

"Do you believe that he would chase us for two days in a steamer if there wasn't something serious the matter?" asked Corny.

"Yes, if he wanted to get this boat," replied Thad.

"Well, I have had enough of this thing. Here we are cruising all over the lake with a thief, running away, and dodging a steamer sent after him; and we are getting into it as deep as he is," blustered Corny.

"Shut up, Corn Winkfield, or I'll smash your head!" exclaimed Thad, leaping to his feet, and moving towards the sceptic.

"None of that, Thad!" interposed Dory, putting his arm between the two belligerent members. "I don't want any fight over it."

The skipper put the helm up, and gybed the boat.

"What are you going to do now?" demanded Corny when Thad had resumed his seat. "I am not going to be carried all over the lake with one who is running away from the officers."

Thad sprang to his feet again, but Dory quieted him.

"I am going back to Plattsburgh to face the music," said Dory.

Corny looked more disgusted than ever.

CHAPTER XVII.

DORY DORNWOOD DECIDES TO "FACE THE MUSIC."

"I'M not going back to Plattsburgh!" exclaimed Corny Minkfield. "My mother will want to know what has become of me by this time."

"What are you going to do, Corny?" asked Dory in the gentlest of tones.

"I am going back to Burlington," answered Corny.

"All right! I don't object," added Dory, as he headed the boat for Plattsburgh.

Thad laughed, and Nat and Dick smiled. Corny talked and acted as though he "owned things;" and the others were rather pleased to see him taken down a peg when he was in this mood.

"You promised to take us back to Burlington, Dory; and now you are going to drag us back to Plattsburgh," growled Corny.

"But you don't want to sail all over the lake

with a thief. If I go to Burlington now, I shall be running away from the officers. I must go to Plattsburgh, and face the music."

"Hurrah for Dory!" shouted Thad. 'Is that the way a thief does it?"

"Hurrah for Dory!" added Dick Short. "That isn't the way a thief does it."

"But I want to go home. I don't want my mother to worry about me," added Corny.

"You called me a thief just now, and I can't run away from the place where they accuse me. I will put you ashore at the lighthouse, or on Colchester Point."

"You might as well put me ashore on Stave Island. I want to go back to Burlington."

"We are bound to Plattsburgh now; and I shall not stop to rest until I have seen the men that charge me with stealing that money," replied Dory very decidedly.

"The man that charges you is in that steamer, and you run away from him," retorted Corny.

"The Missisquoi is hard and fast aground. If I give myself up to him, I shall only have to stay on board of her all day; for he may not get off. I may be in Plattsburgh before he is."

Corny grumbled a while longer, but the skipper took no further notice of him. The course of the Goldwing carried her within a short distance of the stern of the Missisquoi. Captain Vesey and Pearl had tugged at the poles until they saw that it was useless to attempt to get the steamer off in that way.

Pearl was plainly disgusted with the situation. The bow of the boat was as far out of water as when the schooner passed her before, and the efforts with the poles had not started her a hair. When the enterprising extra pilot of the steamer saw the Goldwing coming, he hastened to the stern.

"Come alongside, Dory Dornwood! I will make it as easy as I can for you when we get to Plattsburgh. Take me on board," shouted Pearl.

"I am going to Plattsburgh to face the music," replied Dory.

"Take me with you!" called Pearl.

"I don't want you," answered Dory.

"I can get you off, and make it all right with you."

"No, I thank you," added Dory; and he declined to take any further notice of his persecutor.

For the present the excitement was ended. It was about seven in the morning, as Dory judged by the height of the sun. Thad got out the provisions; and, though there was not much variety to the repast, the boys ate heartily. After the meal some of them went to sleep. Before ten o'clock the Goldwing was alongside the wharf, in the position where Dory had first seen her.

The skipper lowered the sails with the help of the rest of the club, though Corny was still too much disgruntled to do any thing. Every thing was put in order on board, and Dory locked the cabin. Before he had finished, Corny went off alone. Just as the party were going to leave the wharf, a couple of men came down. They walked directly to the boat, as though they had seen her coming up the bay, and had business with her.

"Is this the boat that went off from here yesterday morning?" asked one of the men.

"Yes, sir: this is the boat," replied Dory, hoping that the men's business related to the charge against him.

"Are you the boy that bought her?" continued the man who did the talking.

"Yes, sir: I am the one that bought her and

paid for her," answered Dory. "Do you know of anybody in this town that wants to see me?"

"I can't say I do," said the man, looking at the other one, and laughing.

"There was a little steamer here in the forenoon."

"That was the Missisquoi."

"A man went off in her to look up this boat. Have you seen any thing of the steamer?" asked the man.

"Yes, sir: she is hard and fast aground on the Colchester shoal, near Law Island. The man that went in her to look up this boat was Pearl Hawlinshed. I don't believe in him, and I kept out of the way of him and his steamer."

"How could you keep out of the way of a steamer in a sailboat?"

"I managed it. But I didn't know till he hailed me from the steamer that I was charged with stealing some money from one of the hotels. Can you tell me any thing about the matter, sir?"

"I think we can tell you all about it," replied the speaker. "This is Mr. Moody, the man that lost the money."

"And this is Mr. Peppers, the detective, who is looking up the case," added Mr. Moody.

"As soon as I heard about it, I came back to face the music," said Dory.

"Your name is Dory Dornwood, I learn," said Mr. Peppers.

"Theodore Dornwood is my name, but I am called 'Dory.'"

"Just now we are rather more anxious to find the other man than we are to get hold of you," continued Peppers. "I don't believe there will be much music for you to face, Dory."

"But Mr. Hawlinshed said I was wanted here, and I have come. Is he an officer?" asked Dory.

"He is no officer, and he had no right to arrest you."

"Hallo, fellows!" shouted Corny Minkfield, coming down the wharf: "there is a steamer over here which is going to Burlington, and we can go in her."

"I should rather go in the Goldwing," said Thad, looking at his companions.

"You must be in a hurry about it, for she will be off in a few minutes," added Corny. "We won't get home to-day if we don't take this chance."

"When are you going, Dory?" asked Nat Long.

"I don't know when I shall go. If you have a chance to go, you had better use it," replied Dory.

After a little discussion, the four members of the Goldwing Club decided to improve the opportunity to get home; for Dory could not say that he should go to Burlington that day. All of them but Corny took occasion to say that they believed Dory was all right, so far as the money was concerned; for the detective did not seem inclined to say any thing about the matter beyond the rather encouraging statement he had already made. A few minutes later the skipper saw a small steamer leave another part of the town, and he was again alone so far as friends were concerned.

"I think we had better go up to the Witherill House, and look the case over," said Peppers, after the boys had gone.

"Why do you say there will not be much music for me to face, Mr. Peppers?" asked Dory, as they walked up the wharf. "I am accused of stealing the money, and I don't understand the matter."

"I am sorry Hawlinshed did not come back with you," replied the detective, without answering the question. "In fact, we want him more than we want you."

"Do you want him as evidence against me?" inquired Dory very anxiously.

"We are looking into the case, and finding out all we can. We have some ideas, but we don't say much about them," said the detective.

Dory could not get any thing more out of the officer. They soon reached the hotel, where he was introduced to Mr. Velsey, the landlord, who was informed that the skipper of the Goldwing had come to face the music, whereat he looked very good-natured, and conducted the party to a private parlor.

The landlord wanted to know where Dory had been since he left the hotel the morning before; and he told the story in full of his trip on the lake, and the pursuit of the Missisquoi. The hotel-keeper and the detective were very much amused at the manner in which he had dodged the steamer, and especially when the hero stated that he had left his pursuers aground on Colchester Shoal.

"But, if I am charged with stealing this money, I want to know about it," said Dory when he had finished his narrative. "Pearl Hawlinshed said I was wanted here; and here I am."

"You were about the hotel night before last, were you not?" asked Peppers.

"I was. I was here to see a gentleman who had a room on the next floor. I left between ten and eleven," replied Dory promptly.

"I don't think it is any use to go into that matter, Peppers," interposed Mr. Velsey, when he saw that the detective was disposed to make as much parade over the case as possible. "Come to the point at once."

"Have you any money, Dory?" asked the officer, evidently coming to the point as directed.

"I have: I have sixty dollars and some change," answered Dory, without any hesitation, as he put his hand upon his wallet in his pocket.

"Have you any five-dollar bills?" continued the detective.

"I have two five-dollar bills. The rest of the money is in tens."

"Will you show me the fives?"

Dory produced his wallet, and handed the two bills to the officer. Peppers passed them to Moody at once. The latter shook his head, and handed them back to the detective, who returned them to the owner. The skipper wondered what all this meant, and was very much surprised that Peppers did not ask him where he had got the money he paid for the Goldwing.

"That sets you all right, Dory Dornwood," said the landlord. "I am sorry we made you come back to Plattsburgh, but Hawlinshed was sure you were the one that stole the money from Moody's room. We are satisfied now that another person committed the robbery."

"Then you don't want to send me to jail?" added Dory, with a sensation of the most intense relief.

"Not at all. We didn't know so much about the case yesterday forenoon as we do now. The next man we want to see is Hawlinshed. You say he is aground somewhere in the steamer."

"On the Colchester Shoal: at least he was three hours ago," added Dory.

"That's in Vermont, but I will give you ten

dollars to put Peppers in the same boat with him."

Dory was glad enough to do it. The tables had turned.

CHAPTER XVIII.

DORY LOCKS HIS PASSENGERS INTO THE CABIN.

TEN dollars! And this sum was to be made with the Goldwing. It would pay nearly one-fourth of what she cost, and add ten dollars to the sum he was to have the happiness of giving to his mother.

"I don't understand yet why I am let off," said Dory, after he had recovered from his amazement at the prospect of earning ten dollars.

"You are let off because you didn't do it," replied the landlord, laughing. "I am sorry we accused you, but it looked bad for you at the first of it. Peppers and Moody will tell you all about it after you get into the boat. We have an early dinner ready, and you must dine before you go."

In addition to all this, the landlord invited him to come to his house whenever he was in Plattsburgh, and make himself at home there. The hotel-keeper dined with them, and he asked Dory a great many questions about the boat. Was she a dangerous boat?

"Any boat will tip over if you don't handle her right," replied Dory sagely. "I sailed her across the lake yesterday when it blew a young hurricane, and she is as safe as any boat I ever was in."

The young skipper proceeded to explain what had made the Goldwing so unruly. He had overcome the difficulty, and he was sure that she was as safe as any boat on the lake. He had perfect confidence in her, and he was willing to have her tested in any weather by any boatman on the lake.

"Pearl Hawlinshed wanted to buy her; and he claims to be the greatest boatman on the lake, and knows his way all over it from Whitehall to St. Johns," added the hotel-keeper. "He knows just where the bottom is in every place."

"I think he does," replied Dory, laughing. "I know he found it yesterday and to-day. Any fellow knows just where the bottom is, but he don't always know how far it is from the top."

"I often have parties here who want a boat

and a skipper; and I may be able to turn some business into your hands, Dory," added the hotel-keeper.

"Thank you, sir: that's what I want every day in the week, except Sunday," replied the skipper of the Goldwing.

After dinner Dory and his passengers went to the wharf, and in a few minutes they were standing up the lake. The wind was considerably fresher than it had been in the morning, and the Goldwing made about six miles an hour. The bad reputation of the boat had made some impression upon Peppers, and at first he was very shy when she heeled over under the influence of the smart breeze.

Dory soon satisfied him that the boat would not upset, with any thing like fair treatment. He explained and illustrated the lee-helm business. With the tiller fast in the comb, he allowed the craft to have her own way. At the next gust she threw her head up into the wind, and spilled all her sails. This satisfied both of the passengers, and they manifested no more timidity.

In an hour and a half the schooner was up with Stave Island. The detective had asked the skipper half a dozen times if he could see any thing of the Missisquoi; but the islands had concealed her from view, if she were still on the shoal. A few minutes more would enable him to answer the question. Dory's passengers had plied him so closely with questions since they started, that he had forgotten all about the matter the officer was to explain to him; but the expectation of soon seeing Pearl brought it back to his mind.

"You haven't told me yet why I was charged with taking Mr. Moody's money from his room," said he.

"One reason was, that you were seen about the hotel, near Mr. Moody's room; and the other was, that you had money enough to buy this boat," replied Peppers. "But I was satisfied that you didn't take the money as soon as I got the facts from Moody."

"It was a lucky thing for you, my boy, that I fixed things as I did," added Moody.

"How did you fix things?" asked Dory.

"I have just started the business of making tomato-wine for sickness. I sold two hundred dollars' worth of it in Plattsburgh, part of it to go to New York. The merchant gave me a check for the money, and I went to the bank to cash it. I received forty brand-new five-dollar bills," Moody explained, producing one of the bills. "I am trying to advertise my business all I can; and I had a rubber stamp made, which the agent delivered to me the day I got my money. I went to my room, and stamped every one of those new bills with my business card in red ink. That is the way I know the bills when I see them."

"And that is the reason why you wanted to see all the five-dollar bills I had," added Dory.

"But we had looked over the bills you paid for the boat before," said the detective. "We have been looking for bills with this red stamp upon it since yesterday noon."

"Have you found any?" inquired Dory with interest.

"I found two of them. We have got to the southward of Stave Island now. Can't you tell whether that steamer is in sight now?"

"Yes, sir: there she is, just where we left her this morning," replied the skipper, as he glanced in the direction of the shoal. "I think Pearl Hawlinshed has had a good time there all day."

"How far off is she?" asked Peppers.

"About two miles, but we shall reach her in twenty minutes. Where did you find the two bills with the stamp on them?" asked Dory.

"Can they see us on board of that steamer, Dory?" asked the detective, without heeding the question.

"They can see the boat; but of course they can't tell who is in her two miles off," replied Dory.

"I am afraid I shall have some trouble with Pearl, Dory," said Peppers anxiously. "The landlord was to give you ten dollars if you put me in the same boat with Pearl."

"I think I shall earn the money without any trouble," replied Dory, laughing with delight at the bright prospect before him.

"But, Dory, it makes some difference to me in what boat I happen to be put with him, though you will earn your money all the same," added the officer.

"All I can do is to put you on board of the Missisquoi. Of course I can't put Pearl Hawlinshed on board of this boat if he is not willing to come."

"But I don't want to be put on board of the

Missisquoi," protested Peppers. "There is where the rub comes. I am an officer in Plattsburgh, but not in the State of Vermont. I can't arrest Pearl over here."

"Arrest him! Are you going to take him up?" asked Dory, not a little astonished at this revelation.

"I am not going to do it over here; and he may make me no end of trouble when he sees how the land lays," added Peppers; and at the same time he sat down in the bottom of the standing-room.

"What are you going to arrest him for?"

"For stealing Moody's money!" exclaimed the detective desperately. "I didn't mean to tell you the whole story just yet, but you have dragged it out of me. Drop down here, Moody."

The loser of the money obeyed, though he seemed to be as much in the dark as to the object of the movement as the skipper. Dory was worried at the words of the officer; for, if he would not go on board of the little steamer when he went alongside of her, he might not be able to earn the promised reward.

"What is all this for, Mr. Peppers?" asked

Dory, quite as anxious to earn his money as the detective was to secure his prisoner.

"Can't we go into the cabin, and shut the doors, Dory?" asked Peppers.

"You can; but that would bring the boat down by the head so much that she won't work well. If you want to do that, I will shift the ballast," replied Dory.

"I don't want Pearl to see me until we get him into this boat. It won't do for me to take him out of the steamer over here. I am afraid to do it. Shift your ballast, and then I will fix it up with you," added the officer.

"Fix up the ballast!" exclaimed Dory, who did not care to have any one meddle with the ballast but himself.

"No, no! Fix up a plan to get Pearl into this boat. Don't try to be so thick, Dory," replied Peppers impatiently.

The skipper could not leave the helm to move the ballast, and neither of his passengers knew any thing about a boat. But the men shifted the fifty-sixes under the direction of the skipper. Five of them were carried farther aft, and the passengers took their places one in each berth in the cabin.

The doors opening into the standing-room were closed, but the slide was left open till the schooner came alongside the Missisquoi. The men declared that they were very comfortable in their quarters, and Dory could not see why they should not be. He did not think there was any better place in the known world than the cabin of the Goldwing.

"Now, how are we to get Pearl into this boat?" asked Peppers, with his head at the opening by the slide.

"I don't think you will have any trouble about that," replied Dory. "He wanted me to take him on board this morning, but I believe he will take the boat away from me as soon as he comes on board."

"Don't you be alarmed about that, Dory. I can take care of him when I get him within reach of my hand," added the detective.

"I believe he is as ugly as sin itself, and I think he hates me worse than he does the Evil One himself. I have given him a big run the last two days, and I gave him a chance to find the bottom twice."

"I will look out for you, Dory. I don't want him to know we are on board of the boat till we get over to the other side of the lake," added Peppers. "He will look into this cabin the first thing he does after he comes on board. Can't you give us the key, and let us lock ourselves in, Dory?"

"You can't lock the doors on the inside," answered Dory. "When the slide is drawn, a hasp comes down from it, and all the doors are fastened with a padlock."

"Then why can't you lock us in? You won't tip the boat over while we are in here, will you?" asked the detective, as he thrust his head out far enough to enable him to see the steamer, which was not more than a quarter of a mile distant by this time.

"I will agree not to tip you over; but I can't tell what else may happen, if I take such a fellow as Pearl Hawlinshed on board."

"If you have any trouble with him, all you have to do is to unlock the door, and let us out; and we will take care of you."

"All right! I am satisfied to do any thing you say," added Dory, as he went forward, drew the slide, and locked his passengers into the cabin.

By the change in the position of the ballast the

boat was kept in good trim. She dashed merrily through the water, and in a few minutes more she was describing a circle around the grounded steamer.

CHAPTER XIX.

PEARL HAWLINSHED RESORTS TO VIOLENCE.

"HALLO! is that you, Dory Dornwood?" shouted Pearl Hawlinshed, as the Goldwing came within hail of the steamer. "Come alongside, and take me on board!"

"All right!" replied the skipper of the schooner, as he hauled in the sheets with all his might.

"Take me on board, and I will make it all right with you," continued Pearl, who did not seem to believe that Dory intended to take him on board.

The skipper had brought the boat about so that all her sails were shaking, but she had headway enough to carry her to the port quarter of the steamer.

"Be all ready to jump on board when I come up alongside," called Dory.

"Are you going off to leave us, now that you

have got us into this scrape?" demanded Captain Vesey, springing to his feet; for he had evidently been asleep on the quarter-deck.

"I am going to get a steamer to drag you off this shoal," replied Pearl. "I will come back in a couple of hours or so."

"You may forget to come," added Mr. Button, the engineer. "I think you had better pay me the five dollars you owe me before we part company."

"And five dollars you owe me," added Captain Vesey.

"I don't owe you any five dollars, either of you," replied Pearl blandly, as he was about to leap on board of the Goldwing. "I was to give you five dollars apiece if you put me on board of this boat, and you haven't done it."

"We should have done it if we hadn't let you do the piloting," replied Captain Vesey. "You owe us the money, and you must pay it."

"I think not," added Pearl, as he sprang on the forward deck of the schooner. "You haven't done what I agreed to pay you for."

"Hold on!" shouted Button angrily. "If you don't pay me, I will take it out of your hide."

"You will catch me first, won't you?" jeered Pearl, as he leaped down into the standing-room of the boat.

"Don't carry him off, Dory," added Captain Vesey. "He is the biggest rascal that ever floated on Lake Champlain."

"Keep off, Dory, if you know when you are well off!" said Pearl in threatening tones.

But Dory was anxious to perform his part in the drama; and he filled away on the starboard tack, pointing the head of the boat towards Plattsburgh. His fellow-voyagers did not give Pearl a good character, but this was not a surprise to the skipper. He knew what Pearl was before he had seen him in the daylight.

"Here we are, Dory," said the villain, as he seated himself in the standing-room. "You have dodged me times enough yesterday and to-day, and I am glad to be alone on board of this craft with you."

The skipper did not express his satisfaction that they were not alone, but he felt it just the same. Pearl was ugly, and Dory did not like the looks of him. The new passenger gazed about him, and seemed to be examining the boat for some time. He looked under the seats in the standing-room, and opened a couple of lockers. Then he raised the floor-boards, and looked at the ballast.

When he had done this, he seated himself again. He looked at Dory, and then he glanced up at the sails. He watched the sailing of the schooner in silence for a few minutes. He evidently had something on his mind, and he appeared to be debating with himself as to the manner in which he should open the subject. As his eyes wandered about the boat, they rested upon the cabin-doors. He looked at them a moment, and then went forward, and tried to open them.

"You keep the cuddy locked, do you, Dory?" asked he, as he pulled several times at the doors.

"Just now I do," replied Dory, who had no skill in lying, and no inclination to practise it. "I wish you would come aft, Mr. Hawlinshed. When you are so far forward, it puts her down too much by the head."

"She works very well indeed, Dory Dornwood. What have you been doing to her?" asked Pearl.

"I changed the position of the foremast, and have shifted the ballast," replied Dory, wishing the third passenger would come aft; for he was afraid he might discover the presence of the others in the cabin.

"Do you happen to have the key to this padlock in your pocket, Dory?" asked Pearl in an indifferent tone.

Just then he saw the inquirer drop his head, and put his right ear very near the blinds in the doors of the cabin. But he did not act as if he had discovered any thing. The skipper thought he heard some kind of a noise in the cabin, as though one of its occupants had coughed or sneezed. But he was not sure of it, and the noise was just as likely to have been the dashing of the water against the bow of the boat.

"You spoil the sailing of the boat by staying so far forward," repeated the skipper, with his heart in his mouth.

"Perhaps I do, Dory Dornwood. I asked you if you happened to have the key of that padlock in your pocket," said Pearl, as he moved aft. "I should like to have you answer me if it isn't too much trouble."

"Of course I have the key," replied Dory.

"Suppose you give it to me? I should like to

take a nap in the cabin while we are going down the lake," added Pearl.

"I just said it spoiled the sailing of the boat to have you so far forward. I slept on that seat here in the standing-room last night; and I think you can take your nap just as comfortably there as in the cabin," answered Dory.

There was something cunning and suspicious in the conduct of Pearl Hawlinshed that made the skipper very uncomfortable. He acted as though he was playing a part to accomplish a purpose. The skipper had made up his mind that it was time for him to open the cabin-doors, and thus obtain the assistance and protection of the officer.

"Don't say any thing more to me about spoiling the sailing of the boat, Dory. I know more about sailing a boat than you do," replied Pearl. "You are a cross-grained youth, and you know more than the law allows for a boy of your years. You beat me out of this boat; but you stole the money to buy her, and it was no trade."

The skipper concluded that it was best to make no reply to this charge.

"We will settle that matter at another time,"

continued Pearl. "I believe I hinted to you that I wanted to take a nap in the cabin."

"And I hinted to you that I did not want the boat loaded by the head any more," replied Dory, who was not at all disposed to be bullied, politely or otherwise.

"I prefer to sleep in the cabin, and I want the key of that padlock," said Pearl more decidedly than he had before spoken.

"You can't have it," replied Dory with quite as much decision.

"Do you wish me to throw you overboard, Dory Dornwood?" demanded Pearl, fixing his ugly look upon the skipper.

"No, I don't."

"Then I hope you won't make me do it, for I might be sorry for it; but I must have that key."

"I don't see what you want of the key," added Dory, whose sober second thought was, that he had better not provoke such a dangerous man. "This boat has a bad reputation, and I have to be very careful with her."

"You were very careful yesterday when you ran across the lake in her with the wind blowing a heavy gale," said Pearl with a sneer.

"I will fix a nice bed for you on that seat."

"I want the key!" exclaimed Pearl savagely.

Dory was silent. The key was in his trousers-pocket, where he kept his wallet, containing sixty dollars. His ugly passenger was evidently determined to have the key. Unless he had discovered that some one was in the cabin, he could not see why his persecutor was so strenuous to obtain the key. Pearl was not a large man; but he was very strong and quick, as he had learned in the affair in the woods, when the ruffian had hurled him away from him as though he had been nothing but a baby.

He could hardly get the better of him if Pearl resorted to violence. His .companion in the standing-room claimed to be a skilful boatman, and was not dependent upon him to act as skipper. The situation began to look very serious. Though Peppers must have heard every word that passed between him and Pearl, he had not betrayed his presence on board of the boat. Perhaps it would have been foolish for him to do so, as he was as securely caged as though he had been locked up in the Clinton County jail.

Dory finally decided that the only thing for

him to do was to open the cabin-doors, and thus secure the aid of the officer. But Pearl was watching him as a cat eyes a mouse. Whether the ruffianly passenger would permit him to open the doors was now the question. The skipper got his hand on the key in his pocket, though he did not venture to take it out. At a favorable moment, if any such was presented, he intended to make a rush to the forward deck to effect his purpose.

"There is a steamer bound to the north," said he, pointing to a vessel a mile to the windward of the Goldwing. "Perhaps she would run over, and pull the Missisquoi off the shoal."

"I don't want any thing more of the Missisquoi; and she may lie where she is till she rots," replied Pearl, without taking his gaze from Dory.

"Do you know what boat that is, Mr. Hawlinshed?" asked the skipper, very anxious to induce his companion to look away from him, even for an instant.

"I don't know what steamer that is; and I don't care, unless you should happen to go too near her. In that case, I should object," answered Pearl, without looking at her.

"Are you afraid of her, Mr. Hawlinshed? She looks peaceful enough," added Dory.

"You needn't talk any more. I know what you are trying to do; and you won't do it," said the passenger.

Dory saw that it was no use to wait any longer. Pearl was determined not to take his eyes off the skipper. Dory fussed a moment with the sheets, trying in this manner to distract the attention of the villain. Finally he let go the jib-sheet, and it ran out. With the key in his hand, he rushed forward, as if to secure the rope, but really to unlock the cabin-door.

Before he could reach the doors, Pearl threw himself upon his victim. Dory went down into the bottom of the boat in spite of his best exertions to save himself. His right hand was firmly grasped by his assailant, and the key wrenched from his hand. It was done almost as quick as a flash, and Dory was as powerless in the hands of the villain as though he had been only an infant.

Pearl did not offer to use any more violence than was necessary to obtain the key. When he had secured possession of it, he hurled his victim from him.

CHAPTER XX.

MR. PEPPERS FINDS THE TABLES TURNED.

DORY DORNWOOD gathered himself up after his defeat, and stood upon his legs again. He was mortified at the result of his attempt to release the officer, and improve his situation in the boat. He had thought of using the tiller as a weapon, and now he was sorry he had not done so. Doubtless it was better for him that he had not; for that would only have compelled his assailant to use greater violence, and he might have been seriously injured, for Pearl seemed to be desperate enough to do any thing.

"Now pick up your sheet, Dory," said Pearl, as he went to the helm, and took the tiller in his hand.

Dory did not feel so much interest in the sailing of the boat as he had a short time before, and he took no notice of the order of his conqueror. He looked at Pearl, and saw him deposit the key of the padlock in the depths of his trousers-pocket, which he buttoned up, as though he expected an attempt would be made to take it from him. The new skipper had kept the helm up until all the sails but the jib were drawing full.

"I think I told you to pick up that jib-sheet, Dory Dornwood," said Pearl, in what he doubtless intended for an impressive manner.

Dory had certainly exhibited a considerable degree of prudence under the trying circumstances in which he was placed; but now his stock of that virtue appeared to be exhausted, for he took no notice of the order repeated to him, and the impressiveness of Pearl was wasted. Dory was disgusted at his overwhelming defeat, and he had not philosophy enough to submit to it with good grace. In fact, he was downright mad at the treatment he had received from his last passenger.

He was looking about him for the means of resistance. The long tiller was in the cabin, and he had neglected to take the small one from the rudder-head. As the situation was now, he was disposed to fight; but, unprovided with any sort of a weapon, he realized that he was no match for the villain who had taken possession of the boat.

He looked at the blinds in the cabin-doors. He could put his foot through them; but, if he did, the aperture was not large enough for the officer to crawl through. He began to wonder that Peppers did not say or do something

"If you don't pick up that jib-sheet, Dory Dornwood, it will be all the worse for you," said Pearl, not so impressively as before; for he had found that manner did not operate with the late skipper.

"If you are going to sail the boat, pick it up yourself," replied Dory with more grit than discretion.

At this particular moment the eye of the late skipper rested on a round hard-wood stick which lay on the floor of the standing-room. It was used in shoving down the centre-board when necessary. When he saw it he laid hold of it. He felt stronger in spirit and in muscle as soon as he had it in his possession.

"What are you going to do with that stick, you young cub?" demanded Pearl, rising from his seat.

"I am going to use it," replied Dory, filled with wrath.

If he had waited for some of his wrath to evaporate, he would have done better. With the club upraised, he rushed aft with the intention of attacking his persecutor. He calculated that one blow over the head with the heavy weapon in his hand would depose and dispose of the new skipper of the Goldwing, and restore him to his place again. Possibly it might if Dory had succeeded in delivering the blow. He was angry and excited, while Pearl was cool and self-possessed.

As he struck what was to be the finishing blow of the conflict, Pearl caught him by the arm, and in the twinkling of an eye wrested the club from his hand. He threw it on the floor, and then he jammed the belligerent young man down upon the seat very hard. Dory felt his bones quake as he came down on the board.

"You have got grit enough to fit out a flock of Bantam roosters," said Pearl, still holding his victim by the collar of his coat. "But I don't want any more of this thing, and I won't have it."

Taking a reef-pendant from under the seat, he proceeded to tie the hands of the late skipper behind him. When he had done this, in spite of Dory's struggles, he made him fast to the side of the boat.

"Now, young man, I think you will stay where I put you," said Pearl, as he looked his prisoner over, and saw that he was secure. "You won't make any thing by such stupid conduct."

"What's going on out there, Dory?" called Peppers, who could not help hearing the noise of the scuffle.

"Nothing particular going on just now: it is all over," said Pearl, as he resumed his place at the helm, though not till he had gathered up the truant sheet.

"Why don't you unlock the door, Dory?" continued the officer.

"I can't," answered Dory, whose tongue was not tied, if his arms were. "Pearl Hawlinshed has taken the key away from me, and tied my hands behind me."

"Are you there, Hawlinshed?" asked Peppers.

"Of course I am here. Ask Dory Dornwood if I am not," replied the skipper, chuckling at his own reply.

"What does this mean, Hawlinshed?"

"Well, it means any thing you please, Peppers. So you had passengers in the cabin, Dory; and that is the reason you didn't want to open the cabin," added Pearl.

"Open this door, and let us out, Hawlinshed, if you have the key," said the detective in a mild and good-natured tone, as though he expected the villain to do it.

"No: I think I won't," replied Pearl. "I am afraid you wouldn't behave yourself as well out here as you do in the cabin."

The officer said no more for several minutes. Dory concluded that he was looking over his chances of getting out of his prison. Probably he was willing to admit by this time that the tables had been turned upon him. The owner of the Goldwing could think of no way by which the prisoners could get out. The doors were made of plank, and he could not get at the hinges to operate upon them.

"I think we had better talk this thing over, Pearl," said Peppers, after a silence of several minutes. "We may be able to come to an understanding."

"I don't object to talking it over. I haven't

got any thing else to do; but I am afraid we can't come to any understanding," replied the skipper. "You are a constable, police-officer, detective, and all that sort of thing; and I suppose you went over into Vermont on business. Did you finish it before you were locked into that place?"

Pearl chuckled, and was very good-natured in his remarks; and he plainly felt that he was master of the situation.

"I didn't finish my business; but, if you will open the door, I will end it in a very short time," answered the officer.

"Then I guess I won't open the door," laughed Pearl. "Perhaps you won't object to telling me what your business is in these parts."

"I can't do any thing till you let me out."

"Then you can't do any thing at all. You had better turn in, and take a nap for the rest of the day."

"Do you mean to keep us in here all day, Hawlinshed?"

"Yes: and all night if you don't behave yourself."

Another silence followed, in which the caged

officer was probably considering what he should do next. It was broken by a sudden crash, which startled Dory. He found that something besides the silence was broken. All the blinds in one of the doors were smashed out at a single stroke from the shoulder of the detective. It hurt Dory's feelings to see the beautiful work of the boat reduced to splinters in an instant; but he realized that he was in the midst of a stirring adventure, and the blinds could be easily restored.

"Good!" exclaimed Pearl, as the opening appeared in the door. "You did that very well, Peppers. I was wishing I could leave the helm long enough to do it myself, for I wanted to see who the other fellow was that had taken passage with me. Besides, I think it is a good deal more sociable to see a man's face when you are talking to him."

"Of course you know, Hawlinshed, that you are resisting an officer, and obstructing him in the discharge of his duty?" demanded Peppers, beginning to be a little more demonstrative as he failed to appreciate the humor of the new skipper.

"Of course I understand that I am obstructing

an officer, — a New-York officer over here in Vermont," chuckled Pearl. "By the way, Peppers, have you such a thing about you as a pistol of any kind, — a revolver, a seven-shooter, or any toy of this sort?"

"I haven't any such thing about me. If I had, I should shoot you the next thing I did," answered Peppers petulantly.

"Oh, no! You wouldn't do such a thing as that. It might hurt me," said Pearl with a laugh.

"That is to say" — continued Peppers; and it was plain to Dory that Moody had indicated to him that he had made a blunder in telling the rascal that he had no dangerous weapon.

"That is to say that you haven't any pistol, but the other fellow has one," added Pearl. "By the way, who is the other fellow? It would be a good deal more sociable if you would introduce him."

"His name is Moody, and he will be very glad to make your acquaintance, Hawlinshed."

"If he has got a pistol, it might go off, and hurt one of you in that narrow place; and I think you had better hand it out, and have it properly taken care of," continued Pearl.

"Moody has four pistols, all of them seven-shooters," said the detective, who seemed to be determined effectually to counteract the influence of the blunder he had made.

"Four seven-shooters!" exclaimed Pearl. "He is a walking arsenal. He would sink if he should fall overboard with such a weight of arms upon him; and I think he had better pass them out through the hole you have been so kind as to make."

"He concludes that he may want them, and he don't mean to fall overboard," replied Peppers.

"All right! but let him be very careful with them; for pistols are dangerous things in such a little hole as you now occupy," answered Pearl, who was no simpleton, and was confident that Moody had no pistol, to say nothing of four of them.

A silence of a full hour followed, for neither party seemed to have any plan to act upon. It was plain enough to Dory that the new skipper had discovered the presence of the detective on board of the boat, either before or soon after he went into her himself. A little later he saw a plaid overcoat lying on the forward deck. It was odd enough to betray the identity of its owner, who had forgotten to take it into the cabin with him.

It afterwards appeared that Moody had sneezed twice. This was the sound the skipper heard; and it informed the later passenger that the cabin was occupied, as the coat explained by whom. Two hours had elapsed since the capture of the boat; and the Goldwing was off Cumberland Head, hugging the Grand Isle shore.

CHAPTER XXI.

ANOTHER ELEMENT IN THE CONTEST.

"WHERE are we now, Dory?" asked Peppers, appearing at the aperture in the door, at which he had not been seen for the last half hour, though his voice was heard in consultation with Moody.

"Off Cumberland Head, and close to Grand Isle," replied Dory.

"Is there any thing in sight, Dory?" continued Peppers.

"There is a steamer coming towards the Head. I saw her above Valcour's Island two hours ago; and she has been in at Plattsburgh since that," answered Dory.

"Do you know what steamer it is?"

"I am not sure: she has not been within two miles of us."

"I can tell you all about her," interposed Pearl Hawlinshed with his frequent chuckle. "Why don't you apply at the captain's office when you want any information?"

"I don't think I can depend upon your information," added Peppers.

"I think you can. The steamer is the Sylph," added Pearl.

"I thought it was the Sylph," said Dory.

"She is the fastest boat of her inches on the lake," continued the skipper. "She has run by any of the big steamers, except the Vermont, which is good for eighteen miles an hour."

Dory had seen the steamer before, and he never saw her without having sad thoughts. He always kept away from her if she happened to be in any port where he was. But she was a beautiful craft, and her ordinary rate of sailing was twelve miles an hour; and it was said that she was good for two or three miles more if her owner would only "let her out."

"I don't think there is any comfort in her for you," chuckled Pearl. "She is a private yacht, belonging to Captain Gildrock; and he don't go out of his way to assist poor and distressed fellow-creatures like you."

"How far off is she, Dory?" asked the officer.

"She is half way across Cumberland Bay; and I should think she was four miles off, or thereabouts," answered Dory.

"Just about four: that was a good guess, Dory Dornwood," added the skipper.

"Can't you hail her if she comes near us?" suggested Peppers.

"No, he can't!" exclaimed Pearl sharply. "It would be cruel of you to ask him to do such a thing; for as sure as he makes a sign to that steamer, or to any other craft, I will throw him overboard, with his hands tied behind him."

"It would be cruel of you to do such a thing, Hawlinshed."

"I know it would, and I shall not do it unless you compel me to act in self-defence."

"Where is this thing to end?" demanded Peppers in a disgusted tone of voice.

"Somewhere up in Canada, I guess," replied Pearl. "I don't believe it will end before we get there, and I think we shall be over the line some time to-night."

"Then you intend to take us into Canada, Hawlinshed?"

"Yes: unless we can make some better arrangement. If you prefer to land at some point on Grand Island, I think we could fix it so as to accommodate you."

"How can we fix it?" asked Peppers rather anxiously.

"I have been thinking the matter over, and I believe I have a plan by which I might safely oblige you," said Pearl. "I have concluded not to go back to Plattsburgh: in fact, I don't believe I should be comfortable and happy there."

"I don't believe you would," added the officer significantly. "We should be apt to make it warm for you."

"Why so, Peppers? You and I have always been good friends, and we never quarrelled. Why should we now?"

"We shouldn't, and I don't intend to quarrel with you. But in my private opinion you will spend the greater part of the rest of your days within the stone walls."

"I don't intend to do any thing of the sort; and I don't believe I shall, if I only take good care of you while I have you as a passenger."

"But how can we fix this matter?" inquired the officer.

"If you will put your hands behind you, and then put them out through that hole you have made, I will fasten them together, as I have Dory Dornwood's. I will do the same with your roommate; and then I will land all three of you at Wilcox Cove, or some other good place. How does this plan strike you?"

"It don't strike me at all," protested Dory. "I won't agree to it."

"But, my dear little Bantam, I didn't ask you to agree to it. Your hands are already tied behind you; and, when I have done with you, I shall throw you overboard, if that happens to be the most convenient way to get rid of you. I was speaking to Mr. Peppers, whose hands are not yet tied behind him; and you should not interrupt the conversation of those who are older and wiser than you are."

"I don't agree to the plan. We will turn in and go to sleep, and you can take us where you please; but you will find in the end that this world isn't big enough to hide you from me," replied Peppers.

"Just as you please, Peppers. We shall not quarrel about a little matter like this. I suppose you came over after me. Allow me to suggest that you haven't stated the nature of your business with me," continued Pearl gayly in appearance, though Dory could see that he did not feel half so chipper as he talked.

"I think I won't talk any more at present," replied Peppers. "I can wait till we see this thing through."

"You won't have to wait many hours," answered the skipper, as he looked astern to see if any craft was coming near the Goldwing.

Dory was certain that the skipper was disgusted with the decision of the officer, and that he was very anxious to get rid of his troublesome passengers. But the owner of the boat was delighted with the conduct of the detective. He had been afraid that he would compromise with the villain, and that he should lose his boat, or at least be deprived of the use of her for a long time.

"Where is the Sylph now?" asked the officer half an hour later.

"She is not more than a mile astern of us," replied Dory.

"Is she coming near us?"

"She is headed directly for us."

"And where is this boat?" continued Peppers.

"We are approaching Long Point, and are within half a mile of it. We are inside of Sister Islands, and the Sylph seems to be taking the same course. She acts just as though she was following us," said Dory, who had been watching the progress of the beautiful steam-yacht ever since she first came in sight.

"She does act as though she was following us, don't she, Dory Dornwood?" added Pearl Hawlinshed.

"I have no doubt she is following us," replied Dory.

"Do you know of any reason why she should follow us?" asked the skipper, trying to conceal his anxiety.

"I don't," answered Dory.

"Do you know her owner, Dory?" inquired Pearl.

Dory hesitated. It was a disagreeable topic to him, and he would gladly have avoided it. It was plain enough that the Sylph was following the Goldwing, but Dory could think of no reason why she should do so.

"Do you know Captain Gildrock, her owner?"

asked Pearl again, and with more energy than before.

"I do know him: he is my uncle," replied Dory, who could see no reason why he should conceal the disagreeable truth — for it was disagreeable to him — from the skipper.

"Your uncle!" exclaimed Pearl, apparently startled at the reply. "Do you mean to say that Captain Gildrock is your uncle, you young cub?"

"I mean to say it, and I do say it."

But Dory wished with all his might that the captain was not his uncle, or any other relation.

"He is one of the richest men in this part of the country," added Pearl, looking astern at the elegant steam-yacht.

"I know it; but I don't have any thing to do with him, and I don't think he is coming after this boat on my account," added Dory.

"I suppose you will be glad to get on board of her," suggested Pearl, who had now become quite nervous in spite of his fine philosophy.

"No, I shouldn't. I was never on board of the Sylph in my life; and I shall not go on board of her if I can help it," answered Dory.

"You and your uncle don't seem to be on the best of terms," continued Pearl, as he headed the boat to the eastward, after passing Long Point.

The skipper ran the Goldwing close to the point. The Sylph was within hailing-distance of her at this time; but the steamer had to go a quarter of a mile or more to the northward of the point in order to find water enough for her greater draught. In this way Pearl gained half a mile or more upon her. This enabled him to run the distance to the Gut, which is the strait, or channel, between North Hero and South Hero, or Grand Isle. It was about half a mile wide, between Bow-Arrow Point and Tromp's Point; though there is only a narrow channel, between a red and a black buoy, for vessels that drew over five feet of water at the lowest stage of the lake.

Pearl headed the Goldwing to the southward of the buoys. The Sylph was almost up with the schooner again; and, if the latter had gone between the buoys, the steamer would have overhauled her before she reached them. The skipper became more and more nervous. It was clear to Dory that Pearl was not familiar with the navigation of this difficult place; for he frequently looked over the side of the boat into the water, doubtless to see how deep it was.

"How deep is the water ahead, Dory Dornwood?" asked the skipper, when he seemed to be bewildered, and evidently expected the boat to take the bottom every moment.

"If you are going to sail the boat, you must do it alone," replied Dory after a little hesitation. "I won't do any thing to help you as things are now."

"Goldwing, ahoy!" shouted some one with a gruff voice in the forward part of the Sylph.

But the steam-yacht had stopped her propeller, and immediately began to back. Her pilot knew how deep the water was on the shoal. Pearl made no reply to the hail, and the schooner continued on her course. Off Tromp's Point she struck her centre-board; but, as she was going before the wind, she did not need it, and Pearl hauled it up so that the boat slid over the shallow place.

The man with the gruff voice hailed the boat again; but the skipper did not respond. Pearl hauled in his sheets, and headed the boat to the north-west. The steamer then went through the channel.

"I will play your game upon him, Dory Dornwood," said Pearl, as he put the boat about.

The Sylph stopped her propeller again.

CHAPTER XXII.

THE GAME AMONG THE SHALLOWS.

THE Sylph was bothered by the last movement of the Goldwing. No one knew what she wanted; but she had demonstrated that she was after the schooner, and had business with her. Pearl seemed to be delighted with the success of his manœuvre. He had to drop the centre-board, and beat back. He gave the point a wide berth in standing to the north-west.

"We can keep her going back and forth through the channel till night," said Pearl in high glee. "This is really exciting business, and I enjoy it more than I should a game of cards. I am much obliged to you, Dory Dornwood, for showing me this little trick."

Dory said nothing; for he saw that the game was not the same that he had played early in the morning. There was an element in the contest which had not entered into that between the Goldwing and the Missisquoi; and he thought Pearl was very stupid not to see it. He did not point it out, or even hint at it. He hoped and expected that the interference of the Sylph would restore the schooner to him; and that was all he cared for, though he was quite willing that Peppers should capture and take his prisoner to Plattsburgh.

The steam-yacht started her screw again, and went ahead. In the Gut she came about, and passed between the buoys again. The schooner was almost up with the red buoy when the Sylph passed it, and again the man with the gruff voice hailed the boat. At this moment Pearl tacked, and stood to the south-west.

"I guess she will get tired of this game before a great while," said Pearl, elated with the success of his movements. "She had better give it up, and go about her business."

When the Sylph had passed the buoys, she put her head to the south, and ran down close to the shoal-water. Pearl was so delighted that he was becoming reckless, and he held on to his course until he came within a hundred feet of the steamer. Once more she hailed the boat.

"Is Theodore Dornwood on board of that boat?" shouted the man with the gruff voice.

"If you answer, Dory Dornwood, I'll pitch you overboard!" exclaimed the skipper savagely.

Dory did not answer: he had no intention of doing so before Pearl used his threatening expression. He was not on the best of terms with his uncle; and he did not care to have any thing to do with him, or even to say to him.

There seemed to be a dozen persons on board of the Sylph. But she was a large craft for a steam-yacht, and doubtless some of them were the guests of the owner.

"That will do nicely," said Pearl, as he came about, and let off his sheets again. "The steamer has my permission to go through the channel again. This is better than a game of checkers."

To Dory it was getting rather monotonous. But he did not believe that the people on board of the Sylph would be willing to play at this game much longer. The man with the gruff voice had indicated in his tones, the last time he hailed the boat, that he was becoming impatient at the failure of the Goldwing to answer him.

Dory felt like one who stands between two

fires, and he was sure to be hit by one of them. He was in the frying-pan now, and he did not at all like the idea of being compelled to jump into the fire by the Sylph. He did not like his uncle, her owner; and he did not care to be redeemed from his present unpleasant position by him.

It was bad enough to remain in the power of Pearl Hawlinshed, and to be subject to his caprice; but it seemed worse to be taken out of his hands by Captain Gildrock. If Pearl had not been a villain, in the very act of breaking the laws and committing an outrage upon him and the two passengers in the cabin, he would have been willing to assist him in keeping out of the way of the Sylph. He thought he knew just how this could be done; but, as he could not do any thing to help the rascal, he said nothing. He could not get himself out of the frying-pan, but he meant to keep out of the fire if he could.

"She is coming about," said Pearl, as the Sylph began to stir up the water again with her propeller. "She is going through the channel again to head off the Goldwing. I hope she will have a good time doing this thing."

Dory made no reply to this remark; but he felt

that the end of the adventure was rapidly approaching. Captain Gildrock was not a man to be trifled with, or one to be balked by a sailboat like the schooner. The Sylph went through the Western Cut again. Pearl had run almost up to the red buoy, and was near it when the steam-yacht passed through.

The skipper of the Goldwing started his sheets, and stood off in the shoal-water, where the steamer could not follow him. He chuckled as he did so; and he did not appear to harbor a suspicion that his pursuer could do any thing but run back and forth through the cut.

"I think I shall take my passengers into Canada in spite of the opposition of that big steam-yacht. A mouse or a mosquito can make it uncomfortable for a lion," said Pearl, as he stood off from his pursuer. "Do you know how the water is in this bay beyond the next point, Dory Dornwood?" and the skipper indicated Simms's Point with his hand.

"I do," replied Dory.

"Well, how is the water?"

"It is wet," answered Dory.

"Is that so? How did you find it out?" asked Pearl.

"I felt of it one day."

"If you don't keep a civil tongue in your head, you will feel of it again to-day," added Pearl savagely.

Dory knew there was a half mile of shoal water, deep enough for the Goldwing, but not for the Sylph. But it was shallow off the point; and Dory thought the skipper would get aground before he reached Hyde's Bay. But the water was clear, and Pearl saw the bottom in season to avoid the danger. He stood to the southward then, watching the bottom all the time.

Dory saw that the skipper was making the worst possible move for his own case, and he was rejoiced to see him do it. The Sylph continued farther into the Gut, and finally stopped her screw half a mile east of Simms's Point.

"All right!" exclaimed Pearl, who had half a mile of shoal water between the steamer and the shore on either side of her. "I couldn't have put her in a better place myself."

The skipper looked about him anxiously, as though he was in doubt whether to go to the east or the west. But he had been around the two points west of him, and he seemed to think that his safest way was to stick to the ground with which he had become acquainted. The schooner was half a mile from Simms's Point by this time; but Pearl evidently thought that all he had to do was to return to the westward of the buoys by the way he had come into the Gut, and the Sylph could not come near his boat. He came about, and stood to the north-west.

"We are all right still, Dory Dornwood," said Pearl, as he glanced at the steamer. "She can't come any nearer to us than she is now, and a quarter of a mile is as good as a mile."

Dory kept his eye on the Sylph. The moment she stopped her screw, there was a lively movement on board of her. Orders were given in quick and sharp tones; and presently her two quarter-boats, which were swung on davits, were dropping into the water. This was what Dory had expected her to do before this time.

"What is she doing, Dory Dornwood?" asked Pearl, when he discovered that something was going on upon the deck of the steamer.

"She is doing the next thing," answered Dory, who was determined not to give the enemy any comfort.

"What is she about?" demanded the skipper.

"You have a pair of eyes, and you know how to use them."

By this time the boats began to drop into the water. They were lowered from the davits with the oarsmen on the thwarts, and an officer in the stern-sheets. Pearl could not help seeing what the steamer was doing now. He looked troubled, and he used some needless profanity in an under tone.

"What is going on now, Dory?" asked Peppers, who could not see the steamer through the aperture in the door.

"The steamer is getting out her boats," replied Dory. "She has just dropped one from each quarter into the water."

"Four boats!" exclaimed Peppers.

"No," answered Dory, laughing in spite of his situation. "I didn't say four boats."

"You said one from each quarter; and there are four quarters in any thing, according to my arithmetic," added the officer.

"A vessel has but two quarters, and she has dropped two boats into the water. There are five men in each of them," continued Dory.

"That will do! Dry up, and shut up, all of

you!" interposed Pearl. "I am going to fight this thing out to the end, and I don't want any more talk."

The Goldwing was in behind the land, so that she did not feel the full force of the wind. The lake was calm and smooth behind the point, and the boat moved very sluggishly. Pearl began to be very impatient; but a short distance ahead the surface was ruffled, and she would soon have a better breeze.

The starboard quarter-boat pulled towards Simms's Point, and the port boat in the opposite direction. Whichever way the schooner went, she was sure to be intercepted by one or the other of them. The oarsmen of the boats appeared to be all young fellows. They were dressed in a blue uniform; and all of them wore white linen caps, without visors. The officers showed a profusion of brass buttons on their frock-coats, and wore yacht-caps of white linen.

The boats were white, and were very graceful in their build. The four rowers in each boat pulled a man-of-war stroke. The starboard quarter-boat was ahead of the Goldwing; and the officer in charge of her was urging his men to their best exertions, so as to come in ahead of the schooner. Before the Goldwing could reach the point, she was in position to intercept her.

Pearl scowled when he saw the boat directly in his course. He looked back, and saw the other boat beyond the steamer. He could not help realizing that the pleasant game he had been playing had ended in his being beaten.

"Goldwing, ahoy!" shouted the officer in charge of the starboard quarter-boat.

"In the boat!" replied Pearl in a surly tone: "what do you want?"

"Is Theodore Dornwood on board of your boat?" asked the officer.

"Yes, he is," answered Pearl. "If you want him, you can have him."

At this moment the skipper threw the Goldwing up into the wind, and sprang forward to the place where Dory was seated. Without saying a word, he dragged him off the seat, and proceeded to remove the cord that bound his hands behind him. The prisoner's wrists were numb from the pressure of the line, and he stood up to rub a little life into them. Pearl put the boat about, and headed her for the shore.

CHAPTER XXIII.

HEADED OFF ON BOTH SIDES.

"HOLD on there! What are you about?" shouted the officer, as the Goldwing filled away on the starboard tack. "We want to see Theodore Dornwood."

"I can't sail dead to windward," replied Pearl.

"You needn't sail at all," replied the officer. "Captain Gildrock wished to see Dornwood on a matter of the utmost importance: it is a case of life and death."

Dory was startled by these words. What could his uncle want of him? If anybody was dead, who was it? It might be his mother. His blood seemed to freeze in his veins as he thought of the possibility of such a terrible event. He sprang upon the seat, and hailed the boat at once.

"Is my mother dead?" shouted he; and the agony of his tone was borne across the water with his words.

"No: your mother is not dead. She is quite well," replied the officer, who could not but have been impressed by the despairing tone in which the question was put to him; and he had not lost an instant in relieving the anxiety of the inquirer.

Dory dropped down upon the seat again. His mother was not sick or dead. The current of life began to flow through his veins again. A terrible load was removed from his mind almost as soon as laid upon it. He even began to think that the officer was playing a trick upon him to get him to see the captain of the steamer, whom he had so carefully avoided.

"Give way, my lads!" shouted the officer of the boat, as soon as he had answered Dory's question. "I want Theodore Dornwood. Will you give him up?"

This question was addressed to the skipper of the schooner, which was not more than a hundred feet from the boat.

"Yes, with the greatest pleasure," replied Pearl. "I will put him ashore in here, and you can take him on board.

Dory heard this reply with astonishment and indignation. Pearl intended to put him ashore, and then allow the boat from the steam-yacht to pick him up. If he could keep the boat from coming alongside, and thus prevent the officer from ascertaining the condition of things on board of the Goldwing, the Sylph would trouble him no more. If the business on which she came after Dory was a matter of life and death, Captain Gildrock would not be likely to molest him after he had accomplished his mission.

The Goldwing was now within a hundred yards of the shore. Through an opening in the land she was getting a better breeze, and was making at least four miles an hour. Dory saw that something must be done very soon. He had been released from his imprisonment so that the owner of the steamer should not see that he was in trouble. The boat from the steamer was not hurrying; for the officer seemed to be satisfied with the arrangement Pearl had proposed, to put the boy ashore.

When the steamer's port boat saw that the schooner was cornered, she began to pull towards the scene of action. It had gone but a short distance from the vessel before she changed her course; but she still kept in position to head off the schooner if she attempted to escape to the eastward.

"Get ready to go ashore, Dory Dornwood," said Pearl in one of his mild tones.

Dory made no reply. He was fully resolved not to do any thing of the sort. If he went on shore, and submitted to the villain's plan to escape from his pursuers, he could hardly expect ever to see the Goldwing again. But he considered it the safest way to say nothing about the purpose in his mind.

"You will tell the captain of the Sylph the state of things on board of this boat, Dory," said Peppers, who had no objection to the plan; for he thought Captain Gildrock would make a business of liberating him and his companion in the cuddy as soon as he was informed of their condition.

"Tell him any thing you like, Dory Dornwood, as soon as you get on board of the steamer," added Pearl. "Are you ready to go on shore?"

"If I must go on shore, I suppose I must," replied Dory in a non-committal way. "What is to become of my boat if I go ashore?"

"You can have her again when I have done with her," answered Pearl in a coaxing tone; for, if he could get rid of his pursuers, he cared for nothing else just then.

"Where shall I be likely to find her?" asked Dory in a tone which indicated his incredulity.

"You will find her in Missisquoi Bay, on the northern shore, Dory; and she will be in as good condition as she is now."

"Perhaps I shall find her there," added Dory.

"I will" — But, before Pearl could say what he would do, the centre-board of the boat dragged in the sand on the bottom.

The skipper hastened to raise it, but a few moments later it struck again. Pearl hoisted it up as far as he could, and then kept the schooner away a few points; for she would no longer lie up to the wind as closely as before. In this way he succeeded in getting the boat within about a hundred feet of the shore, and then the Goldwing grounded on her bottom.

The water was not more than three feet deep at the stem of the boat, and it was impossible to get her any nearer to the dry land on the beach. Pearl bit his lip; for both of the boats of the Sylph were pulling towards the schooner, and Peppers would soon have an audience to whom he could tell his story.

"I can't get any nearer the shore, Dory," said Pearl, not a little agitated. "You must jump into the water, and wade ashore."

Dory leaped upon the forward deck, and Pearl probably thought he intended to adopt his suggestion, and wade to the beach. But the owner of the Goldwing had no intention of "giving up the ship" in any such manner. The sails hid Dory from the skipper, so that he could not see what he was doing; and, while Pearl was waiting to hear the splash when he went overboard, Dory grasped one of the stays, and climbed half way to the mast-head before his persecutor discovered what he was about.

"What are you doing up there?" demanded Pearl fiercely. "What are you about?"

"I want to see how far off the shore is," replied Dory, for the want of something more sensible to say.

"Come down this instant, you young villain!" yelled Pearl, whose hope of saving himself was thus endangered by the unexpected freak of the owner of the boat.

"I think I can make myself very comfortable up here for a while," replied Dory, as he placed his feet on the foresail gaff, and passed his arm around the topmast.

"If you don't come down, I will shoot you!" stormed Pearl angrily, as he saw the two boats of the steamer coming nearer to him every moment.

Dory had the average aversion to being shot, and he did not like the sound of the threat. He did not know whether or not Pearl had a pistol, though it was not improbable that he had one. He looked at the approaching boats. One of them was not thirty yards from the schooner, and the officer could hardly have helped hearing the threat of the skipper. The port boat had come near enough by this time to enable Dory to see that his uncle was in the stern-sheets.

"Give way, my lads, with all your might!" said the officer of the nearer boat, speaking with great energy, as though he meant to take a hand in the business on board of the Goldwing.

"Are you coming down, Dory Dornwood?" demanded Pearl, as he stopped on the forward deck of the schooner.

"I think I will come down," replied Dory, who had made up his mind not to run the risk of being shot; but he was satisfied that one of the boats would be alongside the Goldwing before he could reach the deck. "But it isn't so easy to get down as it was to come up," he added, making it as an excuse for the slow movement in coming down to the deck. Dory descended with the utmost caution. He had gained time enough to enable the starboard boat to reach the schooner, and this was all he expected to accomplish by going aloft.

"Come, hurry up, Dory!" shouted the skipper, when he was about half way to the deck.

Dory immediately changed his movement, and began to ascend again.

"What are you about, you young cub? Are you going back again?" cried Pearl.

"You told me to hurry up," pleaded Dory, wishing to gain all the time he could.

"You are a natural fool! Come down, or I'll — do what I said I would," added Pearl, as he glanced at the nearer boat, which was not fifty feet from the schooner.

"All right! I will be with you in a moment,"

answered Dory, as he descended to the deck with a reasonable degree of celerity.

But the boat was alongside the Goldwing as soon as he reached the forward deck. The officer leaped on deck without waiting for any ceremony. Pearl dropped into a seat in the forward part of the standing-room. He evidently realized that he had lost the game he had been playing.

"Which is Theodore Dornwood?" asked the officer as he came on board.

"There he is, on the forward deck," replied Pearl. "He is the most obstinate young cub that ever floated on Lake Champlain. You can take him with you as quick as you please. I don't want any thing more of him."

"What in the world is going on aboard this boat?" asked the officer, as he looked from Pearl to Dory, and then from Dory to Pearl, unable to understand the appearance of things on board. "What have you got cooped up in that cuddy?"

"I thought you wanted Dory Dornwood. Why don't you take him, and not waste any more of your time and mine?" said Pearl impatiently.

"Captain Gildrock wants to see you very much,

Theodore, and there is a place in my boat for you."

"I don't care about going in your boat, and I shall not go on board of the Sylph if I can help myself," replied Dory stoutly.

"There he is again!" exclaimed Pearl, as he glanced at the boat that contained Captain Gildrock. "He is a mule, a sulky dog. If you want him, I will pitch him into your boat for you, and make an end of this business."

Pearl leaped upon the forward deck, intent upon putting his threat into execution. But, as he went up on the starboard side, Dory leaped down into the standing-room on the port side. Pearl followed him, and seemed to have a hope, that, if he could drive Dory into the boat, he might get rid of his troublesome visitors.

"Don't you meddle with the boy, officer," said Peppers through the hole in the door; "and don't you let that man meddle with him."

"What does all this mean? Why are you in there? Why don't you come out?"

Before Peppers could explain, the port boat came alongside, and Captain Gildrock stepped on board the Goldwing.

CHAPTER XXIV.

THROUGH VARIED STRIFE AND STRUGGLES.

CAPTAIN ROYAL GILDROCK was not over forty-five years of age. He was dressed in the uniform of his yacht. He was a good-looking man, of middling height, and rather stout. A single glance at his face would have assured any one skilled in reading expressions that he was a person of great force of character.

"What's going on here, Mr. Jepson?" said he, as he glanced curiously about the Goldwing.

"That is what I was trying to find out when you came on board, sir," replied Mr. Jepson. "Theodore and the man in charge of the boat appear to be at sword's points, and there are two men in the cuddy who seem to be fastened in there."

"What does all this mean?" asked Captain Gildrock. And it was apparent now that he was the owner of the gruff voice.

"I will tell you all about it, sir," replied Peppers, taking this duty upon himself.

"I shall be glad to know, for the skipper of the boat has behaved in the most unaccountable manner."

Dory had retreated to the forward deck again when his uncle came on board, though the captain did not seem to be such a terrible man as one might have supposed from the conduct of his nephew. He desired to keep as far as possible from his uncle.

"I wish you would let me out of this place before I tell the story," suggested the detective.

"Why don't you come out if you wish to do so?" asked Captain Gildrock.

"We are locked in. Hawlinshed took the key away from Dory Dornwood by force, and has kept us prisoners ever since. It isn't a bad place; but it is rather confined for a long stay," added Peppers.

"But I didn't lock them in there," added Pearl. "That was done by Dory."

"Have you the key?" asked the captain, turning to Pearl.

"If you want your nephew, there he is, Captain Gildrock," replied Pearl, pointing to the forward deck. "I don't think you have any right to interfere with my affairs. I will put Dory Dornwood into one of your boats, and you can take him away with you."

"All I want is my nephew; and I don't intend to meddle with what don't concern me," said Captain Gildrock.

"That's the sort of man you are; and I always knew you were as straightforward as a gun," added Pearl, delighted with this statement of the owner of the steamer. "Which boat shall I put the boy into?"

Pearl sprang upon the forward deck, and rushed towards Dory. The boy did not take kindly to this proceeding. He dodged around the foremast, and leaped down into the standing-room.

"Captain Gildrock, this boat belongs to Dory, and Hawlinshed has taken her from him by force," interposed the detective.

"My nephew stole the money with which he bought her," added Captain Gildrock. "I don't think he owns her any more than I do."

"You are mistaken, sir. I don't know where

your nephew got the money with which he bought this boat, but the charge made against him in Plattsburgh is not a true bill. I came over here to arrest Hawlinshed, and that is the reason why I am a prisoner in this coop at this moment."

"You have no right to arrest me in the State of Vermont," protested Pearl, standing on the forward deck. "Captain Gildrock, this is a conspiracy. I had a little difficulty with my father, and this is a trumped-up charge to get me back to Plattsburgh."

This was an entirely new presentation of the case, and Captain Gildrock was confused by the differing statements.

"I am not disposed to interfere in this business. I came for my nephew, and I was astonished and surprised to hear that he was accused of robbery. All I want is my nephew."

"If you are willing to assist a robber to escape into Canada, Captain Gildrock, I have nothing further to say," said Peppers. "If you take your nephew away, and leave things as you find them, that will be just what you will do."

"Of course, I don't mean to render assistance

to any fugitive from justice," replied the captain, more perplexed than ever.

"If you will let us out of this place, I will prove to your satisfaction that Hawlinshed is a robber," added the detective.

"And I can prove that I am the victim of a conspiracy," protested Pearl. "I can prove it by Dory Dornwood, if he will only speak the truth, which he never does, except by accident."

"I am sorry to hear such bad stories about my nephew," added the captain. "I have been told that he was wild, and was going to ruin."

"He can't deny that he had a talk with my father," said Pearl; "and my father and I don't agree very well."

Dory thought they didn't agree at all, but he determined not to say a word on the forbidden topic. He had made up his mind in the beginning not to go on board of the Sylph, and the present aspect of things made him more decided than before. If his uncle and Pearl decided that he should go into one of the boats, he meant to jump into the water, and wade to the shore.

Captain Gildrock was silent, looking from the officer in the cuddy to Pearl. He was considering what he should do. Peppers thought it was a plain case. He desired the visitor to act for himself, after he had looked the case over, and listened to the facts.

"I think I will hear what you have to say, officer," said he, after a few moments' reflection. "It is none of my business; but I want my nephew, though I don't like to do any wrong in taking him away. The only way I can do to leave things as I find them is to let my nephew remain; and I can't do that under the present circumstances. Mr. Hawlinshed, will you unlock those doors?"

"No, sir: I will not!" replied Pearl haughtily. "You are interfering with my affairs, and giving me away to my enemies. If you want your nephew, I will help you get him on board of the Sylph; but you have no business to let those men out when they want to cut my throat."

"I only purpose to look into this matter; and, when I have done so, I shall act as I think my duty requires of me."

"That man is not an officer in the State of Vermont; and he has no right to arrest me here," added Pearl.

"I don't deal in quibbles, Mr. Hawlinshed. All I want to know now is, who has the right in the present situation? If I can ascertain the truth on this point, I don't care a straw whether we are in the State of Vermont or the State of New York. Will you open the doors of that cuddy?"

"No, sir: I will not! And I will not allow anybody else to interfere with my affairs," answered Pearl angrily.

"I am going to open those doors," added Captain Gildrock decidedly.

"I don't believe you will," said Pearl, as he took the key of the padlock from his pocket.

He held it up so that the captain could see it, and then jerked it into the lake. It struck the water about fifty feet from the boat. The next instant Dory dropped into the water, and waded in the direction the villain had thrown it. He had kept his eye on the spot where it had fallen; and the water was so clear that he could see the grains of sand on the bottom.

Pearl saw that his purpose was likely to be defeated by the prompt action of the boy; and, before any one could stop him, he had leaped into the water after Dory.

"That man will drown your nephew if you let him do it, Captain Gildrock!" exclaimed Peppers, as he saw Pearl leap into the water.

But the captain had no intention of being a passive observer of what was about to transpire in the water; for he leaped into his boat, and ordered his crew to back her. In an instant they were pulling with all their might; and the boat had nearly run over Pearl before the captain gave the order, "Way enough!"

"Lay hold of that man," said the captain to the two men who pulled the bow oars.

The young fellows unshipped their oars, and grabbed Pearl with no tender grasp. They threw him down, and then dragged him into the boat.

"Hold on to him, my lads!" added the captain. "Don't let him go."

Pearl struggled for his liberty; but the two young fellows jammed him down in the bottom of the boat, and held him there in spite of his efforts to shake them off.

"This is an outrage, Captain Gildrock!" gasped Pearl, out of breath from the violence of his exertions. "I did not think this of you! I have always heard you spoken of as a fair

"THE YOUNG FELLOWS GRABBED PEARL WITH NO TENDER GRASP." PAGE 264.

man; but you interfere with my business, and hand me over to my enemies!"

"Your enemies, as you call them, are willing to have the truth, whatever it is, shown out; but you are not," replied Captain Gildrock. "If the officer in the cuddy don't make out a case against you, I shall not meddle with you; and you can go to Canada, or wherever else you please. Give way," he added to the two after oarsmen.

The two men pulled the boat, and the captain steered it to the spot where Dory was looking for the key. He had taken no notice of what had been transpiring behind him, but had kept his eyes fixed on the spot where he had seen the key drop into the water. After a few minutes' search he saw it lying on the sand, and picked it up. By this time the boat had come up to him; but he paid no attention to it, and began to wade back to the schooner.

"Come into the boat, Theodore," said Captain Gildrock.

"No, I thank you, sir: I will wade back to the Goldwing. It won't take me but a moment."

The captain thought the boy behaved very strangely, as he had ever since the boats from the

Sylph had come alongside the schooner. But he permitted his nephew to have his own way, and Dory soon climbed over the side of the boat into the standing-room. Taking the key from his pocket, he unlocked the padlock, and threw the doors open. Peppers and Moody crawled out of their prison, and stretched their limbs; for they were rather stiff after being kept so long in one position.

By the time Captain Gildrock's boat came along side, the two prisoners were at liberty. The two bow oarsmen were told to let their captive up. Pearl could not have been more wrathy if he had tried. The pleasant game over which he had rubbed his hands so felicitously had gone against him. He knew that Peppers would get the best of him in the argument, and he had lost all hope. He regarded Dory as the cause of all his misfortunes; and, as soon as he was released, he sprang into the standing-room of the schooner, and rushed upon him.

Very likely it would have gone hard with poor Dory, if Moody and Peppers had not seen what the villain intended. Both of them dropped upon him, and bore him to the floor. He struggled desperately, but foolishly; for he had no chance whatever against Moody, who was a powerful man.

While the maker of tomato-wine held him, Peppers put the irons on his wrists.

CHAPTER XXV.

WIND SOUTH-SOUTH-WEST, BLOWING FRESH.

"I THINK we have him now where we want him," said Peppers, after Moody, under his direction, had tied the prisoner, with the rope that had bound Dory, to the side of the boat.

Pearl Hawlinshed was panting from his effort to escape. He made no reply to the remark of the detective. He felt that he had lost the battle, and any further resistance would be useless.

"I am ready to hear any thing you have to say, officer," said Captain Gildrock, as he stepped into the standing-room from his boat. "If you haven't any case, I shall simply put things where I found them, with the exception of taking my nephew on board of the Sylph."

Dory had his doubts about this; for he was as determined as ever not to put himself into his uncle's hands. He had a sore grudge against him, and he did not want to have any thing to do with him. He had no doubt that the captain would decide against Pearl, for he knew enough of the case to understand that it was a good one. He was already considering in what manner he should get away from his uncle after the robbery question had been settled. He was likely to have a chance yet to use his skill and ingenuity in getting away from the Sylph.

"I am entirely willing to have you do what you think is right after you have heard the facts in the case," replied Peppers.

"Have you arrested my nephew for robbery, stealing, or any other crime?" asked the captain, glancing at Dory, who had retreated to the forward deck; for he wished to be in a situation for action when he felt that it was required of him.

"No, sir: I have not, and he has not been arrested. But I will tell you the whole story, and you will see in what manner Dory is connected with the robbery," answered the detective.

Peppers narrated all that had occurred at the hotel in Plattsburgh, giving all the details that were known in regard to the robbery of Moody's room. He added to it the particulars of the two days' chase of the Missisquoi after the Goldwing, with the landlord's statement in regard to Dory's supposed connection with the robbery.

"Then Theodore was charged with the robbery?" asked Captain Gildrock.

"By Hawlinshed, he was; but that was to cover up his own tracks. As soon as the landlord told me that Pearl accused your nephew of the crime, declaring that he had bought this boat with the money he stole from the room, I got an idea," continued the detective. "I found Moody, and he frankly told the facts. He will excuse me; but he makes temperance wine, though he drinks whiskey himself."

"I don't believe I shall ever drink any more," interposed Moody. "I have been in the habit of drinking considerable whiskey when I went to Plattsburgh: and, after I had done my business, I felt pretty good; for I had sold two hundred dollars' worth of my goods, and I felt like celebrating the event with a little tear. But I was afraid that I might lose my money; and I put one hundred and fifty dollars of it in my bag, keeping the rest in my pocket. I guess that scoundrel saw me put it there."

"It was not till after the Missisquoi had gone off

on her cruise that Moody told me he had marked his money with the rubber stamp," continued Peppers. "Then the landlord told me that Dory had taken the money, and had been seen about the hall, near the room. He had bought and paid for the boat that morning, and I went to the auctioneer. I wanted to see the money the boy had paid. It was five ten-dollar bills; and that settled it that Dory had not paid for the boat with the money taken from Moody's room."

"I am glad to hear that," added Captain Gildrock.

Dory had thought he would be sorry to hear it; but there was a bad misunderstanding between him and his uncle.

"When Dory came back, he showed me the money he had, about sixty dollars," continued Peppers.

"Sixty dollars, besides what he had paid for the boat?" queried the captain.

"That is what he had; but he got eight dollars back from the auctioneer," replied the officer.

"That makes over a hundred dollars," said Captain Gildrock, knitting his brow as though he did not like the looks of this fact. "Where did he get so much money, if he did not steal it?"

"That's the question, Captain Gildrock," interposed Pearl, who spoke for the first time since the narrative was begun. "When you have looked into the matter, you will find that he stole it."

"I don't know where he got it," Peppers proceeded. "That is none of my business. All I know is, that none of the money found upon Dory, and none that he had paid out, was the bills Moody lost."

"But have you no idea where my nephew got so much money?" asked the captain.

"I have not the remotest idea, Captain Gildrock. It don't concern me to know, and I make it a rule to mind my own business. But I did find some of Moody's money in Plattsburgh. One five with the stamp on it was paid for a pistol, and the other for the provisions taken on board of the Missisquoi. Both of them came from Hawlinshed."

"It is a lie!" exclaimed Pearl with an oath.

"Both of the shopkeepers are ready to swear to the identity of their man. Now, I shall take the liberty to do what I have not had an opportunity to do before. I shall search the prisoner. Before I do it I should like to have you look at these two bills, Captain Gildrock. They are the fives paid for the pistol and the provisions by Hawlinshed." And Peppers handed him the bank-notes.

"It will be an easy matter to identify these bills. In addition to the stamp on them, this is the first time they have ever been out of the bank," said the captain, after he had looked at the bills.

Pearl was furious when the officer, assisted by Moody, attempted to search him. Moody handled him very roughly, and he was forced to submit to the operation. Peppers took from a pocket inside of his vest a wallet, which was found to contain quite a roll of new bills. The detective spread a couple of them out on the top of the centre-board casing. The red stamp appeared upon them, and they were exactly like those in the hands of the captain.

"It is a plain case, and I have nothing more to say," said Captain Gildrock. "You have made out your case, and I shall not interfere with your taking your prisoner to Plattsburgh."

"I knew you would be satisfied when you heard the case," added Peppers, as he put the money he had taken from Pearl into his pocket-book, and returned it to his pocket.

"I am entirely satisfied, Mr. Peppers," replied Captain Gildrock, glancing at the sky, and giving a general survey to the horizon to the southward. "I see the wind is hauling to the southward, and it looks like bad weather."

"I noticed that it was calm a little while ago," answered Peppers. "Do you think we shall have a storm, sir?"

"We shall have a good deal of wind, and some rain before many hours, if not before dark. I have to go in at Plattsburgh on my way south; and, if you choose, you can take your prisoner on board of the Sylph," continued the captain.

"Thank you, sir: I should be very glad to return in your beautiful yacht, especially if it is going to blow," answered the detective.

"You may take them on board in your boat, Mr. Jepson. I will take Mr. Moody in mine," said Captain Gildrock. "Theodore, you will go in my boat."

Dory made no reply to this intimation. He

was looking over Simms's Point out into the lake, where a fresh south-south-west wind was now rolling up the white-caps. The captain seated himself in the stern-sheets of the port boat. Moody assisted the officer in placing his prisoner in the starboard boat, and took his place with Captain Gildrock. Pearl, though very sulky and even ugly, offered no serious resistance to the transfer to the boat. With his arms handcuffed behind him, he took the seat in which Mr. Jepson placed him.

The starboard boat, having received her complement of passengers, shoved off; and her crew pulled for the steamer. The port boat was waiting for Dory, who was standing at the bow, behind the foresail. He had the boat-hook in his hand, but he did not indicate in what manner he intended to use it. The fresh breeze was beginning to blow in the Gut, though the Goldwing was sheltered from its full force by the land.

"I am waiting for you, Theodore," called Captain Gildrock.

"I am not going, sir," replied Dory in a mild, but very decided, tone.

"Not going? Didn't you hear me say that I

came down here after you?" asked the captain, evidently much surprised at the boy's answer.

"I can't leave the boat here, sir. It is coming on to blow, and she will drift off," added Dory, struggling to suppress his emotion; for he expected a very unpleasant scene with his uncle now that the issue had been reached.

Captain Gildrock seemed to have no suspicion of the state of feeling to which his nephew had wrought himself up. He appeared to think that his invitation to go on board of the Sylph was enough, and the present attitude of the boy was clearly a surprise to him. It was plain that he had not thought of the schooner, for he was silent when Dory intimated that she was not in a safe position for heavy weather.

"You can furl her sails, and throw over her anchor," said he after a moment's consideration.

"I don't think the anchor will hold her, sir: the sand is as hard as a rock here."

"Isn't she aground?"

"She was aground, sir."

"I will run the boat ahead, and we will drag her farther up on the shoal, and carry the anchor to the shore. Then she will be all right; and you can come up after her in a few days," continued Captain Gildrock, as he directed his bowman to shove off from the Goldwing.

The sails of the schooner were beginning to thrash and bang about as they felt the increasing breeze. The boat had been aground at the bow; but, the moment she was relieved of the weight of the three men who had been on board of her when she grounded, she floated again. Dory had noticed this fact; and, taking the boat-hook, he had thrust it down into the sand, and held her. As the wind freshened, driving her off from the shore, his hold was not strong enough upon the bottom to keep her any longer. But it must be added that Dory did not wish to hold her any longer.

The moment the boat-hook tore out of the bottom, the schooner began to make sternway. Then the jib, the sheet of which was still fast, filled, and the Goldwing whirled around like a top. Then a gust of wind struck the sails, and threw them all over. Dory rushed to the helm, trimmed the sails, and headed the Goldwing across the bay.

CHAPTER XXVI.

DORY DORNWOOD MANŒUVRES TO ESCAPE.

"WHAT are you about, Theodore?" shouted Captain Gildrock, as the Goldwing shot away, heeled down to her gunwale under the blast of the strong wind. "Come about, and run her on the beach."

Dory took no notice of this direction, but grasped the tiller with all his might; and with the short stick it was all he could do to hold her. He dropped the centre-board, and stood to the eastward, evidently to avoid the steam-yacht, which was now giving an occasional turn to her screw to avoid being driven out into the Gut. The starboard quarter-boat had just put the detective and his prisoner on board of her.

Captain Gildrock had put the other boat about; and the four oarsmen were straining their muscles, pulling in the direction the schooner had taken. Mr. Jepson saw what was going on; and, as soon as he had disposed of his passengers, he started his boat to the eastward, with the intention of cutting off the Goldwing as she came out of the bay.

The sky was obscured by piles of angry-looking clouds, and every thing looked like a southerly storm. The sun was now not more than half an hour high, but there would be about an hour more of daylight. The Goldwing was making at least eight miles an hour, and Dory was satisfied that Captain Gildrock's boat could not overtake him. He had headed it to the north-east, so as to take the shortest course; for the Goldwing must soon go to the north, or she would run ashore.

As soon as Dory noticed the change in the course of his uncle's boat, he began to haul in his sheets; for he saw that he was giving the boat the advantage of him, though it was not likely to gain enough to enable it to overhaul the schooner. The port boat was the only one from which he expected any interference. The skipper measured the distances very carefully with his eye. He calculated that he had to make half a mile to reach the point where the starboard boat would intercept him, if at all. Mr. Jepson's boat had to get over at least three-quarters of this distance.

Dory thought his chances were very good. At any rate, he determined to keep on his present course until he found himself mistaken. The Goldwing was tearing through the water at a tremendous rate. Since his passengers left her, she was trimmed down at the stern too much; but this did not interfere with her speed while she had a free wind.

The tiller was a great strain upon him, and it took all his strength to prevent the boat from coming up into the wind. There was certainly nothing like a lee helm in her present condition. As the wind increased in force the farther out he went from the sheltering shore, he was afraid he should not be able to hold her up to her course. If he let her broach to, and spilled the sails, he must certainly lose the race.

Taking the end of the sheet, which was considerably longer than was required, he took a turn with it around the end of the tiller. In this manner he was able to take the strain off his muscles in holding the boat; but at every gust of wind he had to put his helm up, and then let it off. He wanted the long tiller, but he could not leave the helm for a moment to get it.

The Goldwing occasionally dipped up the water over her lee wash-board; and, when she did this, it was necessary to "touch her up," or let her eat into the wind, as she would do if left to herself. The skipper was doing some bold and risky sailing, but he was determined to keep out of his uncle's hands if it were possible. He watched the starboard boat with the most intense interest. He had made up his mind that he had little to fear from her, even if she reached the point where the two courses of the boats met.

If Mr. Jepson put his boat in the course of the schooner, Dory did not see how he could help running over her. The collision would smash the quarter-boat, for it would strike her on the beam; while the schooner was not likely to be greatly harmed. She would strike with her bow, where she was least liable to injury.

As Dory continued on his course, he was satisfied that he was greatly outsailing the boat from which he expected trouble, if he had any. The water was getting rough, which impeded the speed of the quarter-boat, while it did not diminish that of the schooner. Five minutes later he was sure Mr. Jepson's boat would fall astern of him. He was confident of it, but he did not relax his care. The officer was urging his crew to increased exertions, but the oarsmen were evidently doing all they could.

The two craft were rapidly approaching each other. Dory realized that he should not have more than a boat's length to spare, but that was as good as a mile. He tried to keep cool, as his father had often told him he must do when there was any danger in a boat. His heart was in his mouth, and he tried in vain to swallow it; but it seemed to be too big for his throat.

"Hold on, Theodore!" shouted Mr. Jepson, when the two boats came within twenty feet of each other. "Your uncle wants you, and he won't do you any harm."

Dory kept his eyes on the sails of the Gold-wing, and made no reply. He was not afraid that his uncle would hurt him. If this had been all, he would not have run away from him, — at least not before the danger menaced him.

"Hold on, Theodore!" repeated the officer of the starboard boat.

But Dory hauled the tiller up, and kept the sails full, though sundry buckets of water poured over the wash-board into the standing-room at this moment. The Goldwing dashed madly on her course, and the skipper did not even ease her off at this most exciting moment of the chase.

"Hold on! You will surely upset that boat," cried Mr. Jepson, who was no doubt greatly concerned about the fate of the boy who was doing this reckless sailing.

The moment of doubt on the part of the skipper had passed. The stern of the schooner was abreast of the bow of the quarter-boat, and her mission was a failure. Dory had cleared both of the boats; and now he had to contend with the steamer, if with any thing. She could follow him in perfect safety wherever he went. He could not outsail her; and, if he accomplished any thing more, he must get out of her way before she could pick up her boats, and get under way again.

The Sylph could not run into the shoal water where the boats were; and the crews would have to pull back to her against the strong wind, which amounted to half a gale. It was not more than half as bad as it was the day he crossed the lake with a reefed mainsail, and the bonnet off the jib; but then he was not on the open lake, where he could get the full benefit of all that was blowing.

Dory did not wait to see how long it would take for the steam-yacht to pick up her boats, or to see what she was going to do next. He held on his course to the north-east; and ten minutes more, at his present rate of speed, would take him through Eastern Cut into the eastern arm of the lake. He went to the southward and eastward of the red buoy. After he had passed it, he stole a glance at the Sylph. Her boats were close aboard of her, but she had not yet hoisted them up to the davits. When he had made his next mile, and the Goldwing was off Ladd's Point, he could not see her. He was confident that he was two miles ahead of her.

The schooner was under the lee of the Point; and Dory decided that he must, at all hazards, trim the boat, and get out the long tiller. The fifty-sixes which had been moved had not been put under the floor, and he got them ready for a hasty change of position. At a favorable moment he dropped the tiller into the comb well up, and rushed forward with one of the weights. He put it in its proper place, and then attended to the helm until the boat was again in condition to take care of herself for a moment.

By watching his opportunities, he conveyed the rest of the surplus ballast forward; and the schooner was again in good trim. With no little difficulty he removed the short tiller, and inserted the long one in its place in the rudder-head. Though he still used the tiller-rope he had brought into service, it was comparatively easy to steer the boat. He could now work her quicker than before, and more effectually counteract the sharp gusts of wind.

The Goldwing was now out of the Gut; and this arm of the lake, near the channel, between the two great islands, was from three to five miles wide. But she was now under the lee of the west shore, and she would not get the full strength of the blast until she had gone about two miles farther.

By this time Dory had fully made up his mind what to do. His programme for avoiding the Sylph was made out. His natural pride would not permit him to fall into his uncle's hands if it was possible, even at no little risk, to avoid such a catastrophe. He had ceased to wonder what his uncle wanted of him. Captain Gildrock had heard bad stories about him, and he seemed to be prepared to believe them all. He thought it probable that his uncle had heard of his discharge from the steamer, and very likely he had found a place for him. But he did not want his uncle to assist him. This was all he could surmise in regard to the present chase.

To the eastward of the Gut was St. Alban's Bay, which extended about three miles into the land, on the Vermont side of the lake. At the northerly entrance to this bay were three islands. Potter's Island, the largest of them, was over a mile in length. South-west of it, and about half a mile distant, was Ball Island. This island was three miles from Ladd's Point, off which the Goldwing was running with the wind on her beam.

Dory had decided to run across the lake in the direction of Ball Island. He intended to bring into use the tactics which had enabled him to beat the Missisquoi, though he did not expect her pilot to run her aground in any attempt to follow the schooner into shoal water. As well as he could estimate the speed of the Goldwing, she could make two miles to the steamer's three. He had two miles the start of her. When he reached Ball Island the steamer would be half a mile behind him.

Between Potter's and Ball Island the water was shoal, and the bottom rocky. At the ordinary stage of the water, it was from eight to thirteen feet deep; but now it was only from two to seven feet deep. The Sylph would not dare to go through the opening, while Dory was sure of seven feet near the larger island. He had his plan arranged for another movement after this one; but he desired to see how the first scheme worked before he gave much consideration to a second.

Beyond these islands the wind had a rake of five miles, and the roughest water and the heaviest wind must be met after he had passed them. He was not sure that the Goldwing could stand it. Before he was half way across the lake he found she had all she could stand under. But he determined to put her through, keeping out of trouble by letting off the sheet, and touching her up, as occasion might require. He cast frequent glances behind him, to obtain the earliest knowledge of the approach of the Sylph. He was less than half a mile from the southern point of the large island, and she could not yet be seen.

The skipper wondered if she had not given up the chase.

CHAPTER XXVII.

DORY MAKES A HARBOR FOR THE NIGHT.

DORY could not see any reason why his uncle should follow him at all, and especially not why he should chase him in the night and the storm. It seemed to him not improbable that the Sylph had abandoned the pursuit, and gone up the lake.

While he was hoping the chase was ended on the part of his uncle, the Goldwing came up with the south-west point of the large island. Beyond it the sea looked very ugly, and it would shake the schooner up in a very lively manner in the next mile and a half she had to make. Dory did not care to take any needless risks; and, if the steamer had given up the chase, he intended to get under a lee, and anchor till morning.

He looked back once more before the boat reached a position where he could not see the other side of the lake. To his regret he saw the

Sylph just coming into view beyond Ladd's Point. She had not given it up. He wished he had made another half mile, and then she could not have seen the schooner; for she would have been behind the island. She could see him plainly enough now, and she headed for the south of Ball Island.

Having passed through the channel between the islands, the weather there proved to be a perfect muzzler. The Goldwing labored heavily in the angry chop sea, and it was all Dory could do to keep her right side up. In a few minutes more it seemed quite impossible to do so, and Dory let go the mainsail halyards. Whether he was caught or not, he could no longer carry all sail. He had put the schooner before it, but he had to come up into the wind to get in the mainsail.

The young skipper's calculations had been within bounds, and he could afford the time he spent in reducing sail. With more experience he would have taken in sail from choice rather than necessity, for a boat don't sail any faster by being crowded with more sail than she can carry. The foresail was a large one, and it almost becalmed the jib. It was all the sail she needed, and Dory soon saw that he was going faster than at any time before.

A run of a mile and a half more brought the boat up with the extreme end of St. Alban's Point. An eighth of a mile west of it was a small island. Here was another of those channels which the low water rendered available for the purpose of the skipper in eluding his swift pursuer. The channel was about four feet deep; and Dory hauled in the fore sheet, and went through it. Under the lee of the island the skipper found the water quiet. Throwing the boat up into the wind, he ran forward, and hauled down the jib. Then he threw over the anchor, leaving the foresail set.

It was getting dark, and the manœuvring could not be kept up much longer. It would be fifteen or twenty minutes before the Sylph could come up with St. Alban's Point. The Goldwing was behind the island, and he did not think the people on board of her would discover where she was. If they did, she could not follow him through the shoal passage. If she got out her boats again, he could run off to the northward under the foresail. All he had to do was to watch and wait.

He had still a considerable supply of ham and

hard-bread and cheese in the cabin; and, while he watched and waited, he ate his supper. Before he had eaten all he wanted, he saw the bow of the Sylph beyond the point of the little island. She had stopped her screw, and this made it evident to Dory that his uncle suspected he had gone through one of the openings to the other side of the islands.

The skipper of the Goldwing was tired of the chase, but he did not intend to be captured by his uncle. He could hear the escaping steam on board of the Sylph, and he knew that she was not more than a quarter of a mile distant from him. Captain Gildrock would get out his boats again, and send them through the passage, where the steamer could not go. Weighing the anchor, he stood off to the north-west under the foresail only.

Though the wind was blowing almost a gale, the schooner went along very well under the foresail. She had not made half a mile before Dory saw the Sylph standing down the bay again. This movement called for reflection on the part of the skipper. He was not quite willing to believe that his uncle would allow himself to be caught again by the old strategy. If she were going around to the north side of the islands, it was a five-miles' run; and it would take her half an hour to do it.

After thinking the matter over for some time, he concluded that his uncle was using strategy. If he was really going around the islands, he had left the boats where they could intercept him if he resorted to the old dodge. He decided not to be caught in any trap, and therefore he continued on his way to the northward. Ahead of him was Wood's Island, and he changed his course enough to carry the boat to the leeward of it.

It was getting to be quite dark, and the chase could not be continued much longer. It was less than two miles to Wood's Island, and he was soon up with the southern point of it. It was now too dark for him to see the boats, if they had come through from the bay. Dead to windward he at last discovered a green light, which he had no doubt was the starboard signal-lantern of the Sylph.

The steamer was really going around the islands. He watched this light with deep interest, and in a few minutes he made out the red light.

Both the port and the starboard lights were now to be seen, and this indicated that the Sylph was coming towards him. But she was nearly three miles distant, and at present he had nothing to fear from her.

The Goldwing was now up with the cape that extends out from the east side of the island. For half a mile beyond it, was a shoal of rocks and sand; so that the steamer could not come within that distance of the shore until after she had passed this shoal. The coast-line of the island now trended to the west. Taking another look in the direction of the steamer, he found he could see only her red, or port, light. This indicated that she had headed to the eastward, and was going towards the place where Dory had anchored.

The schooner carried no lights, and it was impossible that those on board of the Sylph had seen her in the darkness. She had gone in to the shoals between the large island and the main shore to pick up her boats. Dory was quite satisfied with the present aspect of his case. The darkness would fight out the rest of the battle for him.

A quarter of a mile behind the point on Wood's Island there was a bay, into which he ran the schooner. He hauled the centre-board entirely up, and then worked the boat as far as he could towards the land. When she grounded, he lowered the foresail, and made every thing snug on board. His craft was completely sheltered from the violent wind; but he carried the anchor up to the shore, and buried one of the flukes in the sand.

From the boat he could no longer see the steamer's lights. But, when he had planted the anchor, he went ashore, and walked down to the projecting point, from the end of which, if it had been light enough, he could have seen the whole of the north side of Potter's Island. The port light of the Sylph was still in sight, but in a few minutes it disappeared. Neither of the signal-lights could be seen; and this indicated that the steamer was headed away from Dory's position, or had stopped her screw.

Presently he saw some white lights moving about. He judged that they were lanterns in the hands of the men. Beyond this he could form no idea what was going on. He watched the lanterns for twenty minutes or more. He supposed the steamer was picking up her boats, if she had sent any out: if not, they must be examining the shore in search of the Goldwing. Dory was sure they would not find her, and he felt entirely easy.

About this time it began to rain. The skipper had on nothing but his shirt and trousers, and the rain felt wet to him. He did not like the feeling of it. He had played his part as far as he could that night. If his uncle discovered him in his present retreat, he could not help himself. There was nothing more that he could do to keep out of the way of the steamer. He might as well get into the cabin out of the rain, and take his chances.

As he started to return to the boat, he took a last look to the southward. The lanterns had disappeared some time before, but now the port light of the Sylph came into view again. A little later he saw the green light. Both were in sight at the same time. The steamer, therefore, was coming towards him. He hastened back to the boat, and waded off to her.

Dory did not believe that the Sylph's people could see the Goldwing in the darkness and in the mist caused by the rain. He drew the slide, and crawled into the cabin, leaving the doors open so that he could see out upon the lake. After a while he saw the two lights of the steamer. She was moving very slowly to the northward. The green light disappeared as she came nearer.

The island was less than a mile from the mainland, and the Sylph was obliged to keep half a mile from the shore to clear the shoal. She passed the dangerous navigation, and Dory was strained up to the highest pitch of anxiety as he waited to see whether she was coming in any nearer to his hiding-place. He watched for the green light, but he saw only the red one.

The rain came down in torrents; and the skipper could hear the roar of the gale on the island, though he was completely sheltered from its fury. It was so thick out on the water that he could no longer see the red light, or only caught an occasional glimpse of it. The steamer had gone off to the northward, and this was evidence enough to Dory that his retreat had not been discovered. The excitement was over for that day and that night. The skipper put on the rest of his clothes, and turned in. While he was wondering whether the Sylph would make a harbor, and anchor for the night, or return to Plattsburgh, he dropped asleep. He was very tired, and he slept like a rock till the sun shone into the cabin in the morning.

Southerly storms are of short duration generally, and there was not a cloud in the sky when Dory went out into the standing-room to survey the situation. A gentle breeze was blowing from the west, and the appearance of the lake and its surroundings was as beautiful as the dream of a maiden. It was Sunday morning: he had been cruising for three days on the lake, and he was anxious to get home. But his first desire was to ascertain what had become of the Sylph. She was not to be seen from his position in the boat.

Taking a large slice of ham in one hand, and a quantity of hard-bread in the other, he waded to the shore. From the highest ground, he surveyed the islands and the mainland to the northward and eastward without seeing any thing of the steamer. Walking to the hill in the south of the island, the first thing he discovered, when he got high enough to see over the top of it, was the Sylph. She was headed to the south-west; and

Dory concluded that she had spent the night under the lee of Butler's Island, two miles north of Wood's Island. She was bound through the Gut, and in a few minutes she disappeared from the skipper's view.

CHAPTER XXVIII.

TERRIBLE INTELLIGENCE FROM HOME.

To say that Dory was delighted with the results of his strategy, when he saw the Sylph going through the Eastern Cut of the Gut, would be to state the case very mildly. He sat on the summit of the hill, and ate his ham and hard-bread with entire satisfaction; and, when he had finished it, the steamer was no longer in sight.

He hastened back to the boat, where he ate another slice of ham, with the proper allowance of hard-bread. It was a luxury to be able to eat all he wanted, with no anxiety on his mind. He went to work to put the boat in order for the trip up the lake to Burlington. While he was overhauling her, he came to a bottle half full of whiskey. Possibly the other half of its contents had caused the upsetting of the Goldwing, the fault of which had been charged upon the boat.

He emptied the bottle into the lake, and finished his work on board.

He hoisted the sails; and, getting in the anchor, he shoved the schooner off the beach. Going to the northward of the island, he found that he could just lay his course to the Gut. As the sun rose higher, the wind freshened; and he had an eight-knot breeze all the forenoon. His return was without incident; and as the first bells were ringing for church, he landed at Plattsburgh.

He reported to the landlord at the Witherill House. He thought this gentleman looked very serious, when he expected to be greeted as a successful skipper after his cruise. He had no doubt Peppers had arrived with his prisoner, and the story of his trip must be known. The first thing the hotel-keeper did was to hand him a ten-dollar bill, as his reward for the capture of Pearl Hawlinshed."

"You have earned your money, Dory; and there it is," said the landlord, as he handed him the bill.

"I suppose Mr. Peppers has arrived," added Dory, as he put the money in his wallet.

"Yes: he got back about half-past seven this morning. You had a rough time of it with Hawlinshed."

"Yes, sir: he got the bulge on us at one time," answered Dory, laughing as he thought of the exciting scenes of the day before.

But the landlord did not laugh, as he had always done before. He looked very serious; and the skipper wondered if he had been charged with any other crime, his friend looked so coldly upon him. The landlord pulled out his watch, and then shook his head.

"Have you been to breakfast, Dory?" he asked.

"Yes, sir: I had some ham and hard-bread."

"I should ask you in to breakfast; but I am afraid you ought not to stay here any longer," added the hotel-keeper. "It is nine o'clock now, and you will be late."

"Late? Late for what?" asked Dory, astonished at this remark, which he could not comprehend.

"Late for the funeral," replied the landlord in a subdued and gentle tone.

"The funeral? What funeral?" asked Dory, with his heart in his throat.

The landlord looked at him in silence for a moment, and appeared to be greatly surprised.

"Didn't you know there was to be a funeral in Burlington this afternoon, Dory?" inquired the landlord, almost holding his breath.

"I didn't know any thing about a funeral," answered Dory, trembling with emotion.

"You haven't heard the news? Didn't you know that one of your family was"— And the hotel-keeper paused, afraid of the effect of the sudden imparting of the information to the boy.

"My mother isn't dead, is she?" gasped Dory, clinging to the office-counter for support.

"No, she is not. But another member of your family is to be buried to-day," added the landlord.

"Is it my sister Marian?" groaned Dory.

"No, Dory: it is your father."

The young skipper staggered to a chair, and dropped into it. The landlord hastened to him. His father was dead. Though it was known in Plattsburgh, and had been for three days, that the Au Sable steamer, while in charge of Perry Dornwood, the assistant pilot, had been run over a point of rocks, and wrecked, Dory had not heard of it. Some who could have told him the news did not care to hurt his feelings; others did not know he was the son of the pilot; and many heard of the event, and forgot it the next minute.

"My father dead!" groaned Dory. "And I did not even know that he was sick!"

The landlord did not care to give him the whole of the sad particulars. He was silent, thinking that some friend of the family could discharge this painful duty better than he could.

"That is what my uncle Royal wanted of me, and I have been running away from him," added Dory.

The landlord had seen Captain Gildrock the day before when he came to Plattsburgh to look for the boy; and he supposed he had found him. He concluded that the skipper thought it necessary to take his boat to Burlington, and had therefore permitted the Sylph to go on without him. He was surprised to see him when he came into the hotel.

The Sylph had merely come up to the wharf to land her passengers, and Peppers had only told about the trick played upon him by Pearl. In fact, the captain had asked him and Moody not to mention the fact that his nephew had run away from him. It looked like an unpleasant family matter, and he did not care to have it talked about.

Dory was overwhelmed by the intelligence of the death of his father. It was some time before he recovered his self-possession, and then only when the landlord again reminded him that he might be late for the funeral. His good friend walked down to the wharf with him, carrying a basket of provisions he had ordered for him; but the skipper did not feel like eating now. He took the basket, and the Goldwing was soon standing down the bay.

Of course it was not possible for Dory to think of any thing but the death of his father as he sailed up the lake. He had no particulars of the sad event; but now it appeared that his uncle had been in search of him, and had taken great pains to find him. He regretted very much that he had avoided him, and he thought more of uncle Royal than ever before in his life. He had regarded him as a rich man, who was selfish, and who had neglected his sister, the boy's mother. He had not been in her house since she was married.

At eleven o'clock the Goldwing was off Colchester Light; and it was likely to take a couple of hours more to finish the trip. Dory had eaten his breakfast at five o'clock; and, if he was not hungry, he was faint, and felt the need of food. Mechanically he opened the basket the hotel-keeper had given him. It contained the choicest food from the table of the hotel; and he ate, though rather from a sense of duty than because he felt much interested in the operation. The lunch made him feel better, for it seemed to allay a sort of nervousness that troubled him.

He could not eat all the basket contained. The provision was wrapped up in a sheet of white paper, and then the parcel was enclosed in a newspaper. As he was restoring this last wrapper, something printed in the paper attracted his attention. The article was headed "Suicide of a Pilot."

Dory was almost paralyzed as he read the piece. He was obliged to stop to control his emotion several times before he could finish it. He learned that his father had drowned himself in the lake on Friday, and his body had been found and sent to Burlington on Saturday morning.

For the first time he read of the disaster to the Au Sable. The particulars of that event were reviewed in the article. The steamer had run on the rocks while his father was at the wheel. The paper said that he was either intoxicated or asleep, or possibly both. It was very fortunate that no lives were lost, though several persons had been in great peril.

The pilot was ruined by the catastrophe. The owners of the boat suffered a heavy loss by allowing him to continue in their employ when his habits disqualified him for the responsible position he occupied on board. Perry Dornwood, either from remorse, or the consciousness that he had ruined himself and his future prospects, had ended the life which had been so unproductive to himself and his little family.

It was some time before Dory recovered in a measure from the shock which the reading of this article gave him. He wept bitterly, and reproached himself because he had not been with his mother in the midst of her terrible affliction; but he consoled himself with the reflection that he had been at work for her.

He fastened his boat to a wharf on his arrival,

and hastened to his home. He saw that the Sylph was at the next wharf, and, whatever Captain Gildrock had failed to do for his mother in the past, he was with her in her hour of affliction.

He threw himself into his mother's arms when he reached the house, and wept as he had never wept before. His mother mingled her tears and sobs with her son's. But violent grief usually vents itself, and relief comes. When the people gathered at the funeral, both Mrs. Dornwood and her son were calm. The minister spoke words of hope and comfort to them, and they followed the dead to his grave. Captain Gildrock supported his sister, and certainly no one could have been kinder or more considerate.

They went back to the desolate home. Little was said of the departed husband and father; but all that was said was of his good deeds, and his failings were not mentioned. The day wore away. The door of one state of existence seemed to close with that sad day, and with the next morning the family felt that they had entered upon a new era in their career. Captain Gildrock slept on board of the Sylph, because there was no room for him in the poor abode of his sister.

"When your uncle told me that you ran away from him, I was afraid something terrible had happened to you, Dory," said his mother, after breakfast. "Why did you avoid him?"

"Because I never liked him. While you have almost suffered for the want of food, clothes, and a decent house, he has never done a thing for you. You told me he had never been to see you since you were married. I always looked upon him as a hog," replied Dory with spirit.

"Your uncle Royal and your father could never agree. When I was married, my father and my brother were both opposed to it. They did not believe your father was able to take care of a family. They were right, though I will not speak ill of him who is gone. Your father forbid Royal from ever entering his house. But Royal has offered to help me a hundred times, but I was afraid to accept his aid on account of your father. Now he has offered me a home for myself and my two children in his own house," replied the widow, wiping the tears from her eyes. "He is a good brother."

Dory was both astonished and mortified.

CHAPTER XXIX.

CAPTAIN GILDROCK HAS DECIDED OBJECTIONS.

"UNCLE ROYAL is a different sort of a man from what I thought he was, and I am sorry I kept out of the way when he was looking for me. But I hope, mother, that you don't mean to be dependent upon him or anybody else," said Dory.

"I have struggled hard to get along, and feed and clothe you children," replied Mrs. Dornwood. "If I could get work enough, I could do pretty well; but"—

"I can take care of you, mother; and I shall do it," interposed Dory.

"You, poor boy! What can you do? I heard that you had been discharged from your place on the steamboat," added his mother. "Worse than that: they say you took some money that didn't belong to you."

"Did Corny Minkfield bring that story over here?" demanded Dory indignantly.

"No: your uncle heard it over at Plattsburgh."

Dory told enough of his story to prove that he did not steal the money with which he bought the boat, but he could not tell where he got it. Then he produced the seventy dollars he had in his pocket, and gave that to his mother.

"Why, Dory, where in the world did you get so much money?" exclaimed Mrs. Dornwood, as she took the bills; and the amount was more than she had ever before possessed at one time since she was married.

"I received one hundred and five dollars for a service I rendered to a man near Plattsburgh, and I earned ten dollars by helping the officer capture Pearl Hawlinshed," replied Dory.

His mother wanted to know who had given him the money, and for what; and Dory could only reply that he had promised not to tell. Mrs. Dornwood was not satisfied, and she greatly feared that her son had been doing something wrong.

"I can't tell when I promised not to tell," added he. "The man that gave it to me said that I had saved him from losing a very large sum. With a part of this I bought the Goldwing."

"I have heard all about the Goldwing Club, and so has your uncle Royal," said Mrs. Dornwood. "When he came up yesterday morning, he set about finding you. We couldn't tell any thing at all what had become of you. I supposed you was at work on the steamer till Royal told me you had been turned away."

"It wasn't my fault that I was turned off. Major Billcord blamed me for what was not my fault," replied Dory.

"Your uncle said as much as that, and declared that he should give Major Billcord a piece of his mind. At last Royal came to me to know what boys you played with when you were at home. I gave him the names of all the boys you used to call the Colchester Club."

"They changed the name to the Goldwing Club," added Dory.

"Your uncle found them all, and they told him all about the boat you had bought. He took them with him when he went up to Plattsburgh in his steam-yacht. He wanted them to help him find you," continued Mrs. Dornwood.

"Then Corny Minkfield told him that I was a thief. If he had staid with me, he would have heard the detective prove that I was not a thief. But my uncle heard it all," said Dory.

"He proved that you did not steal the money you paid for the boat from the man at the hotel; and that was all. No one knows to this minute where you did get it."

"If you won't believe what I say, I can't help it," answered Dory, with some indignation in his tones.

"I hope it is all right, Dory; but your uncle is afraid you are getting into bad ways. He wants to do something for you."

"I don't want him to do any thing for me. I am able to take care of myself, and you and Marian besides. With the Goldwing I can make five dollars a day when I can get a party," said Dory.

"You had better see your uncle Royal, and talk with him. He has been very kind to me, and he thinks a great deal of you," said Mrs. Dornwood.

"Thinks a great deal of me!" exclaimed Dory, hardly able to believe the statement.

"That is just what he says. We had a long talk about you yesterday forenoon, after he came back from his trip down the lake after you. He said you were too smart for him, and he told how you had kept out of the way of his steam-yacht. He thinks you have talent, and it would be a great pity to have you go wrong in the world."

Dory was utterly astonished, for he supposed his uncle had a very mean opinion of him. But he was not quite reconciled to having his mother dependent on his uncle. He wanted to be independent, and he had been thinking so much of supporting the family that he was not ready to give up the idea.

"My brother has no family. His wife died before he left off going to sea, and he has no children," said Mrs. Dornwood. "He wants me to keep house for him, and I shall not feel like a dependant. I and my children are his only legal heirs, though he may give his property away by will to whomever he pleases."

"I don't exactly like the idea of living on him," added Dory. "I never did like him, and I can't quite get over the old feeling."

"The old feeling was all wrong, my son. I

should think you would like to live with your uncle, when he has no end of boats, and the finest steam-yacht on the lake," argued his mother.

"I have as good a boat as I want, and I feel sure that I can support the family with it."

Just then there was a knock at the door, and the postman handed in a postal card directed to "Theodore Dornwood." It was from the proprietor of the Witherill House. Two of his guests wanted a sailboat and a skipper for three days from Tuesday morning. He had given his address and terms to the hotel-keeper, and here was the first call for his services.

"Look at that, mother!" exclaimed the young boatman triumphantly. "Three days, fifteen dollars! What's the use of being dependent upon uncle Royal?"

Mrs. Dornwood read the postal, and it looked like an avalanche of business even to her. Dory regarded his fortune as made. He must leave for Plattsburgh after dinner, so as to be sure and be there in the morning. Before this matter was disposed of, Captain Gildrock presented himself at the house.

The owner of the Sylph spoke very kindly to

Dory, and the conversation soon turned to the events of the preceding Saturday. The captain was not yet informed in what manner the Goldwing had finally escaped from him. The young skipper explained it all. Mrs. Dornwood informed her brother of the reason why her son had avoided him, but the captain did not allude to this subject in the presence of the boy.

Dory showed the postal card to his uncle, and said he was going to sail for Plattsburgh after dinner. Captain Gildrock did not like Dory's plan for earning a living. He objected to it in the most decided manner. He did not believe he could make a living in this way, for there would not be sufficient demand for the boat to make it pay.

"But I have a fifteen-dollar job to start with," pleaded Dory.

"That will do very well for one week, Theodore; but you will not find steady employment for the season. But this is not the strongest objection to your plan," replied Captain Gildrock.

"I don't see what other objection there can be to the plan," said Dory, whose heart was set on the scheme.

"Perhaps you will not be able to see it when I mention it; but I think your mother will," continued his uncle. "If you could select your own parties, it might do very well. Many people who indulge in boating are fast livers. You will find that some of your customers are rough characters. You will have a great deal of drinking in your boat, and many men who are willing to pay five dollars a day for the boat are not such persons as I should choose for associates of a son or a nephew of mine."

"I never drink any liquor, beer, or any thing stronger than coffee, uncle Royal," protested Dory. "I found half a bottle of whiskey on board of the Goldwing yesterday morning, and I threw it into the lake."

"Your habits are good now, but it is a question whether they will continue so if you make a business of taking out parties in your boat. You will meet men in their gayest moods, when they lay aside all restraint."

"But I promised the landlord of the Witherill House that I would take out parties when he sent for me," added Dory. "I think I can take care of myself."

"Go in this instance, if you think you ought to do so. I am going up to Plattsburgh in the Sylph this afternoon. I have invited the Goldwing Club to go with me, but I suppose you will be unable to join us," said Captain Gildrock.

"I was going to ask the members to sail down with me," replied Dory.

"Very well: they may go with you, and I will bring them back. I have a scheme in my mind upon which I have been at work this forenoon; but, if you have concluded to do a boating business for a living, I shall have to give it up, at least for the present."

"Has the scheme any thing to do with me?" asked Dory, his curiosity awakened by the remark.

"It has to do with all the members of the Goldwing Club. I have been to see Mrs. Short and Mrs. Minkfield in regard to Richard and Cornelius. But my plan is not yet matured, and I will not say any thing more about it until we see how you make out boating."

"I bought the boat in order to do something to help mother," added Dory. "I didn't give forty-two dollars for it for a plaything."

"Your mother tells me that you have done every thing you could to help her, and have given her all the money you earned. I am very glad to hear so good a report of you, for I have been told that you were rather wild. The only doubt I have in regard to you now is as to where the money came from to pay for the Goldwing."

Dory told all he felt at liberty to tell, but this did not satisfy his uncle any more than it did his mother.

"A man doesn't give a boy over a hundred dollars without some very strong motive; and your mother is not likely ever to know the nature of this mysterious transaction," added the captain.

"I can't break my promise, uncle Royal," protested Dory.

"Some promises are better broken than kept."

Captain Gildrock's residence was about twenty miles up the lake on Beaver River, where he had a large estate. Dory had never been there, though he had seen it from the river. It was decided that Mrs. Dornwood and Marian should go to Plattsburgh in the Sylph, and then go home with the captain, as Dory was to be away for three days.

After dinner Dory went on board of the Gold wing. He had seen and invited the members of the Goldwing Club to go with him, and they were at the wharf when he arrived. In a few minutes they were sailing down the lake.

CHAPTER XXX.

CAPTAIN GILDROCK DILATES UPON HIS NOTABLE SCHEME.

THE first thing Corny Minkfield did was to apologize for his conduct the last day he had been on board of the Goldwing. He was afraid then that Dory had been guilty of some offence which might get them all into a scrape. The skipper accepted the apology, and they were as good friends as ever.

"We are all invited up to Beech Hill," said Thad, when the difficulty between the skipper and Corny had been healed.

"Where is Beech Hill?" asked Dory, who had never heard the name before.

"Don't you know the name of your uncle's place?" demanded Dick Short, laughing.

"I never was there, and I never heard the name before."

"We are going up in the Sylph from Plattsburgh to-night. Captain Gildrock is the bulliest man on the lake," said Nat Long.

"He has got something in his head," added Thad. "He treats us fellows like lords."

"He asked my mother what I was going to do in the way of business; and she told him she should get a place in a store for me as soon as I got through school," said Corny. "You ought to have heard him talk then! He said I was too much of a fellow to be a counter-jumper."

"What is he driving at, Corny?" asked Dory.

"I don't know: he didn't let on; but he has got something in his head."

The skipper found that his fellow-members of the club knew no more about his scheme than he did himself. They had a very jolly time on the trip; but the wind was light, and the Goldwing did not arrive at her destination until nearly dark. Dory hastened to the hotel to report to the landlord, who was very glad to see him.

"I am glad you have come; for there is a gentleman in the house who is very anxious to see you, Dory," said the hotel-keeper.

"Who is it, sir?"

"It is Pearl Hawlinshed's father. When he

heard that his son was in trouble, he hastened back."

Dory remembered that he had a secret to keep; and he said nothing, expressing no interest by word or look in the arrival of Mr. Hawlinshed. He asked about the party he was to take out the next morning, and learned that it consisted of two young men from New-York City. They came in while he was at the counter, and he was introduced to them. They appeared to be very gentlemanly young men, and treated the skipper very politely.

After they had talked a while about the trip, they expressed a desire to see the boat; and Dory went with them to the wharf. They were pleased with the Goldwing, and directed Dory to procure the provisions and other supplies for the cruise. They gave him a list of what they wanted, and Dory could not help thinking of what his uncle said when he found "one gallon of best Bourbon whiskey" among the articles to be procured.

On the other side of the wharf was the Sylph. The young men from New York manifested a great deal of interest in the magnificent craft, and wanted to see more of her. But visitors were not allowed on board, for her owner said he should as soon think of strangers coming into his house as into his yacht without an invitation. While the young men were regretting that they could not see more of the beautiful craft, Captain Gildrock, with Dory's mother and sister, came down. At his nephew's request he invited the New Yorkers on board.

Dory had never put his foot on board of the Sylph before, and he was quite as much interested as his passengers. Mr. Jepson was directed to show them through the yacht; but, after they had looked into the engine-room, Mr. Hawlinshed came down the wharf in search of Dory, who was obliged to postpone his examination until another time.

Mr. Hawlinshed took Dory's hand, but he appeared to be very sad. His son's trouble caused him a great deal of sorrow: in fact, the bad conduct of Pearl was the bane of his life. He told Dory that he had sold his farm in order to get his son away from his evil associates near Plattsburgh. He had come to the conclusion that Pearl was worse than his companions. He had done all he could to save him, and had failed. He was going into a new and sparsely settled region himself, and he had hoped to take his son there; but Pearl would not go.

"He wanted to buy the boat I have," said Dory. "He thinks you furnished the money, or at least induced me to buy her, to prevent him from getting her."

"I knew he wanted to buy the Goldwing; for he had a long talk with me about her the evening I first saw you, just as I was starting for Plattsburgh," continued Mr. Hawlinshed. "I think boating has been the ruin of him. He used to go off with young men of dissolute habits, and I think this was what first led him astray. He insisted that I should give him fifty dollars to buy the Goldwing. I refused to do it, and after much violent talk he rushed away from me. You were present the next time we met, Dory," said Mr. Hawlinshed.

"Perhaps it would have been better if you had given him the money," suggested Dory. "He took one hundred and fifty dollars from Mr. Moody's room, and I suppose he did it so that he could buy the boat."

"I am afraid it would have made no difference,"

replied the sad father with a sigh. "He said he could earn his living, and make some money with her; but it would only have been a career of dissipation for him. I hope you will not permit yourself to be led away while you are running the Goldwing."

"I can't see for the life of me why Pearl did not buy the boat if he wanted her so badly," added Dory. "She is worth ten times what I paid for her."

"He expected to buy the boat for twenty or twenty-five dollars; and, when she went above that, he was mad. He did not believe you could pay for her, and that she would be put up for sale again, and he could get her at his own price. If you had told me you meant to buy a boat, I should have tried to dissuade you from it; but you would not tell me. You said it was your secret."

"I was afraid you might object."

"I should certainly. I should have sent the hundred dollars I gave you to your mother if I had known you meant to buy the Goldwing. You kept your secret, and you have kept mine I suppose; for that terrible scene in the woods appears not to be known to any one but the three who were present at the time."

"But my uncle and my mother believe there was something wrong about that money," added Dory. "I think they believe I stole it, or took it for doing something wrong."

"Is that your uncle on board of the steamer?' asked Mr. Hawlinshed, indicating the captain, who had seated himself with his sister and niece on the hurricane deck. "I wish you would introduce me to him, and I will soon set you right."

Dory conducted him to the presence of the captain and his mother, and introduced him to both of them. Mr. Hawlinshed told the whole story of his relations with his unfortunate son, who was now in jail. He related the particulars of the scene in the woods, and assured them that he had given Dory one hundred and five dollars for the good service he had rendered on that occasion.

"I am very glad to have this matter cleared up," said Captain Gildrock.

"I am happy now," added Mrs. Dornwood. "That money had worried me ever since I heard of it."

"I should not have allowed your nephew to

buy that boat if I had known what he was going to do with the money," added Mr. Hawlinshed. "I think that boats have been the ruin of my boy; and, when they are used to take any and every body out for a frolic, they seem to me to be worse than bar-rooms and other bad places," continued Mr. Hawlinshed.

"My sentiments exactly!" exclaimed Captain Gildrock, looking at Dory.

"Of course I don't think there is any thing bad in the boat itself; but my son was going to take out parties, and make a business of it. Some very fair sort of men leave all their good behavior at home when they go off on these boat-scrapes, and I don't like to have a boy of mine with them at such times."

Dory felt very uneasy during this conversation. He began to have his doubts about the business in which he had engaged. There was nothing bad in the use of boats, but Captain Gildrock contended that a man ought to be as careful in regard to whom he took into his boat as into his house. It was not the boat or the boating to which Mr. Hawlinshed and Dory's uncle objected, but only to the miscellaneous parties he would be obliged to take out in order to earn his living.

Mr. Hawlinshed did not care to have the story of the scene in the woods repeated at this time; for it might make it go harder with Pearl on his trial. But those to whom he had told it were too glad to have Dory's secret cleared up to care any thing more about the matter, though they were full of sympathy for the unhappy father.

Mr. Hawlinshed went back to his hotel. The New Yorkers finished their survey of the Sylph; and she soon left with the Goldwing Club, with the exception of Dory, on board. Not a word had been said in regard to Captain Gildrock's plan.

Dory slept on board of the Goldwing that night. The next morning he started with his passengers. They went over to Mallett's Bay first on a fishing-excursion. When they got there, the skipper was astonished to find that the polite young gentlemen from New York were too tipsy to use the bait and lines he had procured. They drank all they could hold, and then went to sleep. They had not told Dory where to go next, and he anchored to wait for further orders.

At noon they both turned out, but it was only to drink till they were tipsy again. They insisted that the skipper should drink with them; but, when he asked them who was to take care of the boat if he did as they did, they gave up the point. They remained in Mallett's Bay all the first day. The next morning they wanted to go to Missisquoi Bay, and the skipper sailed the Goldwing to that part of the lake. The second day was like the first. On the third they had drank so much that they could not keep up the debauch, and they gambled with props in the cabin.

Dory was disgusted with his passengers; but, when he landed them in Plattsburgh, they were as sober and polite as though they had been with their mothers all the time. The skipper received his fifteen dollars, and that was all the satisfaction he got out of the cruise. He returned to Burlington the next day, and spent the afternoon in looking for another party at the hotels.

There was no more business that week. The next week he got only a half-day job, taking a party of ladies and gentlemen across the lake. Three dollars was all he made that week; and he was beginning to be discouraged when he received a postal from the Witherill House. It was a fishing-party to Mallett's Bay. The young gentlemen from New York were saints compared with his present passengers. They got crazy drunk; and, when a shower came up, they threatened to throw the skipper overboard because he anchored the boat to avoid a squall. Dory was afraid of his life, and five dollars a day was no compensation for the misery he endured.

Another week satisfied Dory that the business was a failure, for he did not obtain a single fare. He went to his mother, and told her he had had quite enough of it. He was ready to sell the boat, though the Goldwing Club had fine times in her when she was not engaged; and there were plenty of fine times for them. He had been offered a place in a dry-goods store, and he was willing to take it.

"I think you had better see uncle Royal before you take the place," said his mother. "I have never sailed in the Goldwing, and Marian and I would like to have you sail us up to Beech Hill."

"What does uncle Royal want me to do, mother?" asked Dory, who suspected that the captain and his mother had something on their minds.

"I don't know. You must let him speak for himself," replied Mrs. Dornwood.

The next morning Dory took his mother and sister into the Goldwing, and sailed up to Beech Hill. His mother had to act as his pilot, for he did not know how to take the boat from the river to the estate. Leaving Beaver River, he followed a narrow and crooked stream, though it was very deep, till he reached a small lake, on the shore of which stood the house of Captain Gildrock.

The party received a warm welcome, and Mrs. Dornwood stated the business that had brought them to Beech Hill. Seated in the library, the great question was opened for discussion and settlement.

"Go into a store!" exclaimed Captain Gildrock. "There are more merchants and traders in the country now than can get a living, and mercantile life is a desperate struggle in these days. Be a mechanic, Theodore."

"A mechanic!" exclaimed Mrs. Dornwood.

"A mechanic, Patty," added the captain decidedly. "The first thing a boy wants is an education, and the next is a good trade. I have been thinking of this subject for years. Now I am going to tell you about my scheme. I want to help supply the country with good, educated mechanics."

"I don't think mechanics need much education, Royal," suggested Mrs. Dornwood.

"There you are mistaken, Patty. What this country, especially the Eastern and Middle States, needs more than any other class of men, is educated mechanics, — skilled labor. Too many boys want to be shopkeepers, and wear fine clothes."

"I should like to be a mechanic, uncle Royal," said Dory.

"So would the other members of the Goldwing Club," continued Captain Gildrock. "Now I will tell you about my scheme. For the last year I have had enrolled about a dozen of the young fellows of this vicinity as volunteers on board of the Sylph. Jepson and I have been instructing them in seamanship and mechanics. Jepson has instructed them in the science of the steam-engine, so that they know all about the building of one, though they haven't the practical skill to build one. They have acted as engineers and firemen of the yacht; and every one of them is competent to run a marine engine, or any other."

"Those were the young fellows that were pulling your boats that day, were they not?" asked Dory.

"They were, Theodore. The only men I employ on board are the cook and a waiter, but I have required every one of these young men to learn to do plain cooking. All of them have served a term in the galley. I am captain, and Jepson is the first officer, of the Sylph. I have taught these students how a vessel or a boat is built, how to sail a boat or a ship; I have instructed them in navigation, and required them to get the latitude and longitude of every principal point on the lake; I have taught them how to heave the log, and keep a vessel's dead reckoning; I have required them to survey portions of the lake, and make charts of their work. They have been greatly interested, and they have profited by their opportunities. Not one of them has rich parents, and all of them must soon earn their own living; and you may be sure that not one of them will be a shopkeeper, a lawyer, a doctor, or a minister."

"I should say that was first-rate," added Dory,

with enthusiasm. "I suppose some of them will be sailors."

"About half of them have a desire to go to sea, and some of them have got places as engineers, oilers, and firemen. Two of them will run stationary engines. I have done with them; for most of them were obliged to go to work, and take care of themselves."

"Won't they go in the Sylph any more?" asked Dory.

"I have done all I could for them, and so has Jepson. So far as our teaching facilities are concerned, they have learned out. My new scheme contemplates doing the same work in a more thorough and practical manner. The trouble with my past crew was, that I did not have them more than one day in a week; though we occasionally put in a week at a time in vacation, as at the time when I went down the lake to find you. That was their last cruise; and they were discharged, so to speak, two weeks ago."

"Are you going to ship another crew like that, uncle Royal?" inquired Dory eagerly.

"Not as I did the last one. I am going to establish a sort of practical school," replied the captain.

"I should like to ship for one," added Dory.

"I have had my eye on the members of the Goldwing Club, for they are just the boys I desire to take. I don't want any sons of rich men. I want those who need looking after, and I think the Goldwings fill the bill. I shall take only half a dozen to begin with. I want them all to come to Beech Hill, and live here. I won't take them on any other terms. I shall look out for their book-learning; but, at the same time, the boys must become carpenters and machinists. They must work at these trades, and others as the plan is enlarged. I shall keep them busy all day long, from one end of the year to the other. We shall build houses, boats, bridges, wharves, and eventually steam-engines, and various kinds of machinery. I expect to see the time, though it may not be for ten years, when we can build a steamer like the Sylph, including her engine, and about every thing on board of her."

"It seems to me you are laying out a great undertaking, Royal," said Mrs. Dornwood.

"If I can make honest and useful men out of even half a dozen boys like the members of the Goldwing Club, who are in danger of going to ruin, my money will be well spent. A kind Providence permitted me to make a fortune before I was forty-five, though I had to work hard for it. I have no wife, no children. I think I can realize more enjoyment from a portion of my money in this way than I can in any other. It is wholly to my taste and fancy, this scheme of mine; and it holds out to me a thousand times as much pleasure as any business enterprise I can think of. That's the whole of it, Patty."

"It is a good deal better to use your fortune in that way than to risk it in speculating in stocks, as a great many rich men do," added Mrs. Dornwood sagely. "But it seems to me that you mean to work the boys very hard, — from morning till night from one year's end to the other."

"But I mean that they shall have abundance of recreation. They will be the crew of the Sylph; they shall have hours for their games; they shall have plenty of reading, both for recreation and for study: and if they don't enjoy themselves from morning till night, and from one end of the year to the other, it will be my fault as well as their own."

"When will this thing begin?" asked Dory.

"I intend to make a beginning by the first of September next. Patty, you must move up to Beech Hill at once, now that Theodore has given up the boating-business. You may tell the other members of the Goldwing Club all about my plan, my boy. I have seen the parents of some of them. They can see their friends as often as they please, and spend Sunday at home if they wish. If you see any other boys like those of your club, you may report them to me; but don't ask them to come to the school, or hold out any inducements to them. I must pick the boys myself."

"But I must take time to sell the boat I bought," suggested Dory.

"You needn't sell her, Theodore. I have no sailboat of just her size, and she may be useful. Now keep cool, and remember that it will take some time to get the school into running order, and fit up our shops. But we will begin the scholastic work at once, so that the boys will not lose what they have learned in school."

Captain Gildrock talked about his plan till dinner-time; and the skipper of the Goldwing was so delighted with it, that he felt as though he wanted to fly. He went all over the estate at

Beech Hill, and examined the boats with a professional eye. In the middle of the afternoon the family started for home in the schooner.

In the evening Dory went to see all the members of the Goldwing Club, and their eyes were as big as saucers while they listened to the notable scheme of the retired shipmaster. They were quite as enthusiastic as Dory over the idea. The next day their mothers had consented to their joining the embryo school, which was as yet without a name.

Mrs. Dornwood gave up her house, and at the end of a week Dory sailed the family up to their new home at Beech Hill. The other boys were to come up on the first day of September, which was two weeks hence. Though the Sylph was without a crew, the captain made up one, and they visited various parts of the lake on business and for pleasure. Mr. Jepson, who had first come to Beech Hill as the engineer of the steam-yacht, resumed his old position. Dory was wheelman, and a couple of men who worked on the place did duty as deck-hands. Dory liked this position as pilot even better than sailing the Goldwing, though his services were often in demand as skipper of the schooner.

For more than a year Dory had felt as though he were all adrift in the world. He wanted to get some steady work by which he could help support the family. He had not succeeded very well. But now, for the first time since he had come to think for himself, he did not feel as though he was All Adrift in the world. He was settled with the future before him, and he was resolved that it should be filled with good work.

He read in the newspaper that Pearl Hawlinshed had been sent to the state prison for a year and a half; and he could not help thinking what a terrible thing it was for a young man who had a kind and devoted father, whose existence had been bound up in him, to come to a bad end.

Dory Dornwood was no longer "All Adrift;" and the Goldwing Club were anchored with him. In another volume we shall look in upon them in their "Snug Harbor" as "The Champlain Mechanics."

www.ingramcontent.com/pod-product-compliance
Lightning Source LLC
Chambersburg PA
CBHW031854220426
43663CB00006B/624